# OUTRAGEOUS COURAGE

### What God Can Do with Raw Obedience and Radical Faith

## KRIS VALLOTTON
## & JASON VALLOTTON

**Chosen**
*a division of Baker Publishing Group*
Minneapolis, Minnesota

"This remarkable story of a courageous woman fully yielded to God will stir you on to greater depths of love and obedience. I was greatly inspired by her tenacity and passion to carry God's Kingdom to the least of these, on earth as it is in heaven. I pray that as you read this book, you, too, will completely lay your life down for the One who is worthy, Jesus."

Heidi Baker, Ph.D.,
founding director, Iris Global

"Written on these pages is the tangible authentic power of God that will help you step into another dimension of understanding what it means to lay down your life, take up the cross and follow Him. As Tracy Evans takes you into her life with Jesus, you will find yourself saying, 'God, I want to know You like that!'"

Dr. Ché Ahn, senior pastor, HRock Church,
Pasadena, California; president, Harvest International Ministry;
international chancellor, Wagner Leadership Institute

"Tracy's reputation preceded her. I had heard from Bill Johnson about her several years ago. I am so excited that her story of faith, compassion and miracles is being written. I believe this is a faith-building book where there is more drama than in a novel, but this one is true. I encourage you to buy and read a copy of Kris Valloton's new book about the life of Tracy Evans."

Randy Clark, founder and president,
Global Awakening and the
Apostolic Network of Global Awakening

# Contents

# Foreword

There are few people in the world I admire as much as Tracy Evans. To put it more accurately, there are few people in the world I fear as much as Tracy. I realize that may not sound biblical to some, or even healthy, yet the most honest expression of my heart is "I fear God in Tracy." It is not because she has an intimidating presence or imposing personality. She always comes as a servant to all. But she is one of the most thoroughly converted individuals I have ever met. Her life is an offering, continuously poured out for the glory of God. She is what I call "God-possessed." *Everything* is about and for her Lord and Savior, Jesus Christ. No exceptions.

*Outrageous Courage* is a brief record of Tracy's very full life. But even that is a gross understatement. It is really about God, His love for people, His goodness and His incredible work in and through one yielded vessel. It is certainly not about a perfect person. That becomes clear pretty quickly. It is about a perfectly wonderful God who is capable of doing infinitely great things through finite people. That is the brilliance of Tracy's story. And that is the brilliance of this book. It is filled with intrigue, danger, faith, miracles and God's mighty deliverances.

There is no question, it is God who is amazing. But those who walk in this level of obedience look a lot like their Father— *amazing!*

I was moved when I saw the title for this book. It does not seem possible to come up with a better title for a book about Tracy than *Outrageous Courage*.

Never has there been a time where supernatural courage is more needed than today. It is no longer optional. One of the most wonderful, almost unexplainable byproducts of reading this book is that people will grow in courage. These kinds of God stories impart something wonderful into the heart of every hungry person who reads them. They supply the people of God with a fresh understanding of God Himself, as His ways are revealed in His works. They also invite us to embark on a similar journey, just to see how outrageously the Lord is prepared to touch humanity through any yielded vessel willing to be used to display His extreme goodness. I am convinced that books of this nature are some of the most important books being written.

I have watched Tracy's life for more than thirty years now. She has been consistent from day one. Her growth is astonishing, especially when you see the environment she willingly places herself in, time and again. She illustrates that the greatest growth in Christ happens not in a sterile, classroom-type environment, but in the dirty places of this world, where life and death are everyday realities, where if God does not intervene, we will fail, even die. This is the lifestyle Tracy has chosen to live. It is the lifestyle of His greatest pleasure.

*Outrageous Courage* will not disappoint. Read it hungry, and you will finish it hungrier. It does more than satisfy; it launches the reader on a quest—a partnership for something new. It is bound to be used by God to raise up a new breed of believer—loving, simple, relentless and filled with faith; for nothing is impossible with God.

Many thanks to Kris Vallotton for insisting that her story get written. While Tracy continues to live a full expression of the Gospel, she has lived more for Christ in the years recorded than most people could live in several lifetimes.

Bill Johnson, pastor,
Bethel Church, Redding, California;
author, *Hosting the Presence*,
and co-author, *The Essential Guide to Healing*

# Acknowledgments

Sincere thanks to Kris Vallotton, Jason Vallotton and Allison Armerding. They made the dream of this book a reality. May the Kingdom of God continue to advance, until the King Himself comes!

Tracy Evans

# Introduction

*The Adventures of Tracy Evans*

It all began one summer day nearly thirty years ago, when I heard a motorcycle pull up outside our little country church in Weaverville, California. I bridged the threshold of the church door just in time to see a young, skinny tomboy awkwardly hopping off the bike. Little did I know that the course of my life was about to be altered forever.

"Hi, I'm Tracy Evans," she said with a warm smile.

I extended my hand to greet her. "My name is Kris."

We exchanged pleasantries for a few minutes, but Tracy seemed guarded and uncomfortable as our conversation grew more personal. I found myself quickly intrigued by her. She seemed a little mysterious . . . the thought actually crossed my mind that I might be meeting a secret agent or a spy. Something about the way she carried herself captivated me. I bombarded her with questions to try to figure her out; she must have felt as though I were interrogating her. She managed to duck most of my inquiries, but this only fueled my curiosity.

Despite her private manner, before long Tracy and I became very close friends. She spent many evenings at our house, where we talked about God deep into the night. I had never met anyone so hungry to know Jesus. She seemed possessed by the love of Christ. And although she did not look tough or hard, she was the bravest person I had ever met. Tracy literally had no fear of death. Hanging around with someone who truly did not care if she died was a challenge, to say the least. She would go out in the middle of the night and look for transients under a bridge or in some dangerous alley just so she could talk to them about Jesus. I mean, the girl was nuts! Many times she would lead people to Christ and then take them home to her humble, one-room apartment and let them stay there. She would stay at our place, so we would often wake up in the morning to discover that Tracy was sleeping on the couch in our front room.

Every day was an adventure with Tracy. She was not only brave; she had the kind of faith in God that I had only read about in the Bible. Living around her was like hanging out with David and his mighty men. Consequently, miracles happen through and around her nearly every day. The truth is, I would not have believed her stories if I had not witnessed many of them myself.

Eventually, Tracy gave her apartment to the homeless and moved in with our family. She shared a bedroom with our two young daughters and had a huge impact on all our children. In fact, when Jaime was fourteen years old and Shannon was twelve, Tracy talked us into letting them smuggle Bibles into communist China—just one of the countless terrifying situations she put us in with her exploits.

"God will protect the girls," she argued at the time. "And if they die, they'll be giving their lives for something that really counts!"

Of course, Tracy never thought these feats were a big deal, which only served to make me feel like a coward. Our daughters, however, shared Tracy's zeal. We never tried to talk them into some radical adventure; they were the ones pushing us to let them go! On their way home from China, they called to try to talk us into letting them spend the rest of their lives helping the Chinese people. I finally had to put my foot down to get them to come home. To this day, Jaime, Shannon and our son Jason are all in full-time ministry—a tribute to Tracy and her adventures.

## Through the Years

Many years have passed since that fateful day when that young, courageous gal came into our lives, but nothing has changed with Tracy. A couple of years ago, the phone rang while I was in church. I looked at the caller ID and realized it was Tracy calling from Africa. I slipped out of the sanctuary to answer her call.

"Hi, Tracy! How are you doing?" I pressed.

"I'm doing fine," she replied joyfully. "But I called to ask you to pray for my Mozambican friends."

I could hear a "zinging" noise in the background, so I asked, "What's that noise, Trace?"

"Oh, that's what I'm calling you about. There's a riot outside our house. The police are shooting at everything, and the bullets are flying in all directions. All my Mozambican staff are lying on the floor, scared to death that they're going to die," she explained, her calm tone oddly dissonant with the facts she was communicating.

"What! What the heck are you doing?" I shouted.

"I'm sitting at the table, drinking tea with one of the other missionaries. But I need you to pray for the town because they're in full riot. The police are shooting hundreds of rounds into the air to scare the rioters off. But the rounds that go up eventually come down, and some people have been killed. The situation is escalating right outside our door. Would you pray that God would give them peace, please?"

"Tracy, get your butt on the ground," I insisted.

"I'm fine," she replied with confidence.

I prayed for her and hung up the phone, shaking my head.

## Making Waves

Tracy Evans's life has had such an unbelievable influence on me, my family and my friends that I wanted to introduce her to the world. Her courageous exploits remind me of people like George Washington, Winston Churchill and Joan of Arc. Short of biblical characters, I struggle to find anyone with whom to compare Tracy and her passion for God. (I am sure there are some such people, but I do not personally know any.) I have been threatening to tell her story for more than a decade, but Tracy has resisted drawing attention to herself. Even after giving me permission to tell her story, she has worked hard to deflect any praise away from herself in this book. After months of wrangling with her, I finally convinced her that God would be glorified through her real story and that many people would be inspired, encouraged and transformed by her life.

My son Jason and I decided that in order for Tracy's story to have the kind of impact on others that it has had on us, it needed to be told in the first person—in her own voice. You will therefore read Tracy's stories in her own words in chapters 1 through 11. Our team recorded and transcribed more than a week of interviews with Tracy, which we then composed into a literary account. Jason and I worked hard to make sure that both the facts and the "mood" of all Tracy's stories and exploits were accurate and complete.

I believe her story has the potential to be the next *Pilgrim's Progress*—a graphic depiction of the journey of discipleship that can teach and inspire everyone who reads it. Instead of being an allegory, though, this book and all its stories are true and unembellished. We hope and pray that Tracy will have the kind of impact on you that she has had on all of us. Put on your seat belt and let the journey begin!

# 1

# Taken Hostage

It was a moonless night. From the beach, my companions and I gazed long at the starry sky looming over the South China Sea, seeking to discern the smallest wisp of a cloud or the tiniest ripple of waves—any sign that another typhoon would descend as I attempted to cross the channel from the Philippines' capital island of Luzon to Oriental Mindoro.

I had decided this would be my last go at making a sea voyage during the harrowing Philippine typhoon season. Nearly all my cash was gone, spent on two aborted ferry rides that would have made most people stick to terra firma for life. Few hours of my life have been more horrific than those I spent clinging for dear life to a pole, deafened by the eerie din of groaning steel and screaming winds as wave after wave swamped the deck, flinging passengers and debris all over the place. The first ferry barely found its way back to land, but we had been blown so far off course that I had to hitch a ride back to our original port. The other ferry ended up marooned on a sandbar till the storm passed and fishing boats could come to our rescue. Yet I had decided to give the crossing one more try. This time I had thrown in my lot with a few men who wanted to deliver a load of thatch to the island. We had chartered a motorboat (much faster than a ferry), agreeing that at the first hint of a storm, we would turn tail and head back.

The Milky Way shone down unhindered by any cloud and sparkled back up at us from serene, glassy waters. The tide was at its highest, covering the sandbars that would otherwise hinder our passage to the open sea. It was all clear. My companions and I climbed aboard with our luggage and the load of thatch and chugged away in the still night. As the miles of sea peacefully slipped beneath us, we relaxed and began to chat and laugh, enjoying the starry beauty all around us.

After a few uneventful hours, we saw shoreline stretching out before us. As we began to close the last few hundred yards between us and that white line, suddenly the boat rose and fell. A sandbar swell. Then another. Then . . . a big one. The kerosene lantern launched free from its post, spilling and igniting kerosene all over the bottom of the boat. In seconds, the flames caught the load of thatch and roared to life, engulfing the boat in a raging inferno.

There was nothing for it—I abandoned ship. The South China Sea is known to be sharky, but I had to take my chances. When I came up for air, I saw figures silhouetted against the flames, still trying to get the burning thatch off the boat. "It's no use!" I yelled. "It's too late! Jump!"

One by one, the men plunged into the water. As the last remnants of the boat burned and sank away forever, we swam together toward shore—and toward another fire. Someone had seen our flaming boat and kindled a beach fire to help us find our way through the dark night.

Apart from the skirt and shirt I was wearing, everything I owned—my backpack, my Bible, my guitar, even my flip-flops—was now at the bottom of the ocean. My companions were no different, and one had suffered nasty burns. But we were all alive.

The island people who met us on the beach helped us drag our half-drowned selves from the water, brought us to the fire to dry off and gave us food and dry clothes (I was twice as big as most of them, which made the latter a bit of a challenge). The only thing they had for the burnt man was homemade moonshine, which he gratefully sucked down until his pain became bearable. But when we asked the islanders about how to get back to the capital island, they said they could not help us. Apparently, our boat burning was a bad omen about our fortunes at sea. After my experiences in the previous few weeks, I was almost inclined to agree with them.

A couple of our new island friends did offer to guide us to the nearest town—an eleven-day walk through the jungle. We set off the following week. Thanks to the rainy season, the ground was soft under my bare feet. I was the only woman and the only Westerner, and I was definitely the least seasoned for long jungle treks. Despite having weathered extreme conditions and a barrage of illnesses in the previous five years, while serving as a missionary medic on a garbage dump outside Manila, I was still unprepared for the likes of this jungle challenge. We walked until I could not walk anymore, made a meal of whatever our guides could find (mostly tropical fruit and grubs) and stretched out on the jungle floor to sleep.

In the morning, I awoke to find my body aflame with insect bites. It seemed every mosquito and bug on the island had been invited to a banquet hosted by my twenty-nine-year-old flesh. Somehow they found even more to chew on the next night. By the third morning, I could not find a square centimeter of skin that had not been bitten. My eyes were swollen slits, and my lips were enormous. But I pressed on, shuffling into town on the eleventh day—a bloody, filthy, miserable mess.

My shipmates and our guides soon bid me farewell and left to find their way home. I approached some villagers and introduced myself in Tagalog, the national language. Despite my appearance, I was still discernible as a white woman and therefore was a novelty, so they were curious about me and what I was doing in their town. I explained that I was a missionary. They happily nodded. They were Catholic, they said, and it just so happened that I had arrived on the very day one of their family members was having his firstborn son christened. "Come with us!" they invited.

A little later, I found myself dirty and bedraggled amidst a procession of family members and their neighbors, all immaculate in their Sunday best. After the baptism, the family invited me back to their shack for dinner. At the baptism, I had noticed a confusing mix of Catholic and indigenous practices common among the island tribes, so I asked them if they knew the good news of the Gospel. As I had anticipated, they had never really met Jesus. I introduced Him, told them what He had done for them and invited them to know Him. All twelve family members prayed with me to receive Christ.

"Stay with us," they all said. "Stay and teach us more."

How could I refuse? Besides, I had no other option. Almost overnight, I became not only a member of this family of twelve (you grow close to twelve people pretty quickly when you all live together in a one-room hut!) but also one of the town. Word spread that I was a kind of nun who had come to serve them, and that worked perfectly for me. I freely began to talk about Jesus with everyone I met. The little church meeting in our home soon overflowed with new believers, so I started a second, and then a third, in other homes.

One day I visited the town prison and met the warden. He gave me carte blanche to minister to the prisoners. Being a medic, I also began treating people wherever I could and managed to track down some donated supplies from a hospital in one of the bigger towns farther inland. Before long, I had gone completely native—I lived with the people, ate with them, dressed like them and was becoming more conversant in their language. It was exhilarating. The months flew by like a dream.

One day I was sitting on a bus, on my way back from the bigger town where I had picked up more medical supplies. As I mused over the events of the day with satisfaction, suddenly, without warning, I had a vision. I saw myself escaping a warlike scene and leaving my new family and beloved town. I could not believe it.

"Really, Lord?" I asked Him. "But everything is going so well." I was simply shocked. It could not be right, could it? I decided to sleep on it . . .

. . . only to be awakened the next morning by gunshots ripping through our village. The unmistakable sound jerked me from peaceful sleep, and I knew at once what they meant. *They're here!* I thought.

The villagers had told me all about the Communist guerillas lurking in the jungle. Occasionally, the distant rumble of their machine guns had reached our ears. But until that morning, they had never yet breached the Philippine national military lines set up between us.

Crouching in my hut, I could hear the distant screams of the villagers as the guerillas rousted them from their homes, announcing that they were now in charge. The rebels soon arrived at our house. My native dress could not hide my Western face. They quickly recognized me as American and hauled me into their commandeered headquarters for questioning.

Stories raced through my mind. I had heard that these rebels depended much on the support of smaller villages such as ours. One of their favorite tactics was to attack a military envoy and steal their weapons and uniforms. Then, disguised as the military, the rebels would pillage the village, raping and looting as they went along. Afterward they would return to the jungle, don their rebel gear and reenter the same village, this time posing as heroes who had just defeated the evil military and had come to offer the people their protection.

These rebels were not to be trifled with. My one hope was that I could somehow convince them that I could help them win favor with the village and that I could assist them medically. I needed to prove myself much more valuable to them alive and untouched than otherwise.

The guerilla commander and one of his men started my interrogation. "Who are you? You CIA? What're you doing here?"

"I'm a medical missionary," I replied. "I'm American, but I am not CIA. I'm here doing some medical work, and I'm the only one providing Western medicine in the town. If you hurt or kill me, the villagers will blame you for taking away their only medical provider."

I went ahead and made my offer: "I can tell that many of your men are sick and wounded. They're malnourished." I pointed at the dirty bandage on the commander's leg as I spoke. His movements clearly showed that he was in considerable pain. "You have a wounded leg. I can see that if you don't get treatment soon, it will go gangrenous. You'll either lose your leg or your life. Then what? I'm a medic, though, and I can help you."

The commander nodded to the other man, and they left the room to talk it over. All I could do was pray. I had ignored God's warning to leave, and I knew I was sitting in the consequences. I apologized and asked for His mercy, committing my life once again into His hands.

Finally the men returned. The commander said, "We'll keep you—if you take care of us."

*Thank You, God.* "I will," I said. "But I also need to continue caring for the villagers. They'll help you if you let me help them."

"How do we know you won't use all your supplies on the villagers?" the rebels countered.

"I'll keep track. I promise to treat one of your soldiers for every ten people in the village. But I must be the one in charge of the supplies. If you take them away, I cannot help you."

The commander considered, and then nodded yes.

"I also lead three churches here," I added. "The villagers will respect you if you let us continue to meet and worship."

Another nod. Apparently my offer to save the commander's leg was having a positive effect on our proceedings. But he still had more questions for me. By their drift, I discerned that he was hoping I might be useful to them as a bargaining chip with the military. I was not too sure about that . . . I was a lone white girl with no money and few connections. I was not even registered with the American embassy in Manila. But I was happy to let the rebels think otherwise.

At last the commander sent me home with armed guards, agreeing to let me stay with my family in the village under house arrest. It was not like I could have run far anyway—we were on an island. After I explained the arrangements to my family, I set out for the guerillas' quarters to start making good on my end of our deal.

When the rebels saw me approaching, clutching my bag of supplies, they sprang into action. Sneering, one shoved his machete in my face. "What do you think you're doing here?"

"I'm your new medic," I said, holding up my bag. "Your commander sent me here to help you."

The rebel grabbed the bag and tossed it to his companions, who began rooting through its contents and throwing hostile looks back at me. "We'll see," he said. "If you're lying, we'll rape you—then we'll kill you."

I could see that most of these fierce-faced guerillas were no more than teenagers, mostly likely pulled from Catholic villages just like this one. So I squared off with them and said, "So you're going to rape a nun, huh? What are you going to say to God about that?"

That line of reasoning somehow worked with them. The leader put his gun down, took my bag from his friends and gave it back to me.

"All right," he said. "You can help us."

The men needed help. They were all teeming with parasites, and many were wounded. One by one I cared for them, offering the Gospel along with bandages and medicine. Over time, several rebels prayed with me to receive Jesus. A few months later, some of them even escorted me to Oriental Mindoro's capital city to pick up some Bibles. But with every brick I laid to build trust between me and my captors, I was conscious that one false move on my part would tear it down in a heartbeat.

When we could, my family and I talked about possible plans for my escape. As long as things seemed to be going along all right, though, I avoided the topic. Such talk was very risky. I knew I would only have one chance to escape; if I were caught, they would make an example of me and I would be killed. I did not want to endanger my family or the other villagers by involving them in an escape plot. Yet as I neared my one-year anniversary on the island, it became increasingly clear that I needed a plan.

The military had begun to seriously escalate its attacks on the rebel guerillas. The rebels offered me up for a hostage exchange, only to find, as I had suspected, that I had no value to the military whatsoever. My medical supplies also dwindled rapidly as the military blockaded the delivery roads from the capital city and more and more wounded rebels in need of care returned to the village. My value to the guerillas was depreciating, and at the same time, they were growing more reckless and unpredictable as the surrounding tensions mounted. They began getting drunk almost every night, often breaking into fistfights. Hatred, fear and violence hung palpably in the air.

Finally, my family took me aside and said, "Tracy, you can't stay. You have to try to escape. Please let us help you."

They had a plan. After hearing it, thinking it over and praying, I agreed. We picked a night, made our preparations . . . and waited.

On the appointed moonless night, I quietly said my farewells and blessed these precious ones who had truly become my brothers and sisters. Then it was time. While some of my family members created a diversion for the rebels standing guard outside our house, I crept out of a back window and took off running into the blackness toward the town prison. A men's prison, we reasoned, was the last place anyone would look for a white woman. I ran the entire mile as fast as I could. My friend the warden met me at the prison gate and brought me inside, once he made sure that I had not been followed. We lay low for a couple hours, until one of the prison guards arrived to escort me to a little boat destined for the capital island.

The guard and I arrived unseen at the beach just before dawn. The sea was still, just as it had been on that fateful night one year before. I climbed into a waiting boat, and as we pulled out, I waved to the prison guard, one of the many islanders who had risked their lives for me that night. I was leaving as empty-handed as I had come . . . but with a story of God's remarkable faithfulness that would strengthen and encourage me for a lifetime.

# 2

# Conquered by Love

Long before I was a Christian missionary, I was a confused teenage runaway desperately looking for my place in this world. After growing up in a more or less dysfunctional home in Los Angeles, with my father in prison and my mother working double shifts to support me and my brothers, I was eager to jump ship after graduating high school. Mom had remarried, and life with a new stepfather was . . . difficult for all involved. My grandmother gave me her old car for my sixteenth birthday, and I ran away from home and lived out of that car while earning my associate degree at a junior college. (I lied about my age to get in.)

Two days before my junior college graduation, a drunk driver totaled my car, leaving me unemployed, homeless and desperate. I had been working weekends in a restaurant to support myself through college, but cash was too tight, so I lived in my car and showered in the girls' gym. When my car was totaled, I was therefore both homeless and unable to get to work. With no place of my own, I began thinking that

31

the Army seemed like a good option. However, being only seventeen by then, I needed parental permission to enlist. Without much hesitation, I took an Army recruiter with me back to the home I had left and convinced my mom to sign me over to the military.

## Who Is My Enemy?

A lot of people struggle in the military, but I loved it. Beyond providing room and board for homeless, foolish teenagers like me, it provided structure, discipline and clear leadership. The Army was physically and mentally demanding; there is not a lot of compassion for the faint of heart in boot camp. But I was athletic and stubborn, so the physical and intellectual training was a welcome challenge. Shortly after completing boot camp, I found myself working in military intelligence and looking to climb the proverbial ladder of success. At that stage of military history, West Point had just begun to open its doors to women—an all-too-tempting challenge I just could not pass up—so I applied in hopes of pursuing a career as an Army officer.

While I waited to hear back from West Point, I continued my work in military intelligence. My platoon was made up of a diverse group of individuals from all over the country. We needed a leader who could piece us together like an intricate puzzle and provide clear direction. After a short time, a woman named Julia Carson (not her real name), whom I had also gone to boot camp with, was chosen to do just that. Unfortunately, this particular woman was a Christian, and I detested Christians. I decided to make it my personal goal to harass the faith out of her, hoping to break her down. The more I pushed, the stronger Carson became. As my mockery of her continued, I noticed that deep inside, I was beginning to secretly admire her courage and strength. My original tactic to weaken her was turning on me.

One particular day in boot camp, we were ordered to make a ten-mile march with our weapons and fully loaded packs. As if that were not enough, it seemed the summer weather had partnered with our officers just to punish us. The heat and humidity were stifling. Not long into the exercise, many in my platoon began to collapse, fainting or vomiting in the oppressive heat. At one point, I came up alongside Carson. She was chanting "the blood of Jesus, the blood of Jesus" over and over. I thought it bizarre, but afterward noticed that she was one of the few who finished the course that day.

Carson would often tell us, in a very natural and unassuming way, what would happen in the next few days. To our surprise, things would take place exactly as she had said. I had no grid for understanding the prophetic at that point, so I began to think she was psychic. *This woman has some kind of connection to another reality*, I figured.

Despite the hardships, Carson was full of joy and practically glowed in the dark. Every night she read her Bible on her bunk. I became obsessively curious about what was so important in that book that she had to read it every night. One day when everyone was out of the barracks, I snuck in and grabbed her Bible. Holding it in my hands, its pages fell open like a trap door, just as if it had been rigged, to these verses: "You have heard that it was said, 'You shall love your neighbor and hate your enemy.' But I say to you, love your enemies, bless those who curse you, do good to those who hate you, and pray for those who spitefully use you and persecute you" (Matthew 5:43–44).

I slammed the Bible shut. I could not believe it! Carson and I were being trained in all the different ways we could kill our enemies. We were learning to use M16s and light anti-tank artillery as weapons of destruction. Hating our enemies made it easier to exterminate them! How could a soldier go through this training while reading a book that commands people to love their enemies? It did not make any sense. My mind was spinning, searching for some kind of explanation. *This is either absolutely ludicrous,* I reasoned, *or it takes some kind of supernatural power or divine intervention to do that.*

Either way, I was going to find out. I decided that the way to tease out the truth was to test it by becoming Carson's enemy! My passion to harass her returned with a vengeance, and my plans for tormenting her grew to new proportions. I booby-trapped her locker before inspections. I messed up her uniforms. I would lie awake at night just thinking of ways to get her into trouble and humiliate her. Whatever I did, I always made sure she knew I was responsible. I did everything I could to threaten and intimidate her, though not to the point of physical violence. I never laid a hand on her, just in case she did have some kind of power. If her God existed, I did not want to get on His bad side.

This went on for five months. Without fail, Carson responded in grace, love and mercy every time I harassed her. She never retaliated. In fact, she did not seem the least bit intimidated. Things finally came to a head late one stormy winter night. I went for a run, and when I came back to the barracks, I found her ironing my fatigues and polishing my boots. I was stunned by her kindness. She not only refused to retaliate; she deliberately treated me with kindness. She was clearly a military strategist in the warfare of love, and my heart finally admitted that she had won. Feeling completely defeated, I sat on my bunk and asked her, "Why are you doing this?"

With no inkling about why I tormented her and not knowing that I had read that very verse in her Bible, she quietly answered my question by explaining, "Jesus commanded us to love our enemies." She described how God loves us in spite of our ignorant sin. Up to that point, I had never allowed her to say a word to me directly about God or Christianity. I did not want to hear any religious theology. I had been exposed to Christianity growing up, but it had all been talk, never something real or demonstrated. I had no idea it could be like this—a supernatural manifestation of love to the unlovable, hope to the hopeless and joy to the joyless.

As I listened to Carson that night, I felt as though I were being thrust a hundred miles per hour into an undeniable, mind-boggling reality. For the first time in my life I felt love, and unbelievably, it was coming through this wild story of the cross. Jesus' life for mine! I broke down weeping. The superior warfare of love had finally penetrated the many layers of anger and hardness in my heart, and all I could do was lay down my arms and surrender.

As I wept, Carson quietly put an arm over my shoulders and asked if I wanted to know this One who loved me like no other. I nodded. "All you have to do is ask," she said.

Between broken, snotty sobs, I surrendered and invited Jesus into my life. When I got up the next morning, I seemed to be living in a new world. It was as if the stars had aligned or something. I did not realize that I had changed; I thought everything around me had changed. The grass was greener and the sky bluer—my whole world was blooming! I thought, *I'm on another planet. What's happened?* Three days later I was baptized in the Holy Spirit. My life was changing so rapidly that I actually thought I was going crazy. But I thought, *If this is crazy, it's wonderful and I'm in!*

### Crazy in Love

Have you ever seen someone in love? People in love are ridiculous! They are fun to watch, but you have to admit, they are terrible to work with. Most of the time they are so pre-occupied with their beloved that it is almost impossible for them to focus. They are always in a daze. And people in love cannot help but share it. Well, I was now crazy in love with Jesus, and I wanted everyone to know. I became totally obsessed with telling the other soldiers about Him. Sometimes I would go down the hallway in the barracks and knock on every door. I would even sit patiently at the latrine and wait until a soldier sat down inside. Then I would think, *I've got at least thirty seconds to talk to her through the stall door.*

I was all zeal and no wisdom, cramming Jesus down everyone's throats. Some were turned off, but several received the Lord. Before long, Carson and I were leading a small group of soldiers into something of a mini-revival on post. The chaplain gave us a key to come to the chapel any time we wanted, and every day, as soon as we finished our duties, we were there . . . sometimes all night long. I still have a photograph that shows a sea of our Army boot toes and our hands in the air, as all of us lay on our backs on the chapel floor and worshiped the Lord.

After a while, this newborn passion began to interrupt our training. We became preoccupied with loving each other and lost our military focus. Our superiors began to break up our group and scatter us around. Carson, now a dear friend, ended up losing her position in military intelligence. Fortunately, she was reassigned as a chaplain's assistant, which was ideal for her.

I was even more disruptive than she was, so they actually pulled me in and sent me to a psychiatrist. I guess my continual tears of joy and incessant witnessing looked a little unbalanced. However, nothing else mattered—all I cared about was leading people to Christ. I led my lieutenant, a woman who was supposed to discipline me, to the Lord, and she ended up joining the chapel choir. Then our commander received Jesus. I was so in love I even tried to get the psychiatrist saved! Unfortunately, that did not go over too well.

Eventually, my base had seen enough of me and my love-drunk behavior. Initially, the Army sent me to another post three thousand miles away. It did not matter to me; it was just another place where people needed Jesus. Before long, however, my new commander called me in and threatened to send me to the brig if I did not shape up and get in line.

That shocked me, because I still loved the military, the soldiers and what I was doing. I had even received my appointment to West Point, and I thought I was on track with my military career. But soon after that confrontation, I received word that West Point had withdrawn my appointment because my behavior looked too extreme. I was crushed. I had climbed so high, only to fall so far.

Finally, I was called in and offered an honorable discharge. Initially I did not accept it, but two weeks later they called me back and said, "That's not an option." Taking the hint this time, I accepted and got ready to move on to something new. Looking back now, I know I could have gotten a Section 8 discharge for the mentally unfit. But my performance had remained strong overall, and I was not being malicious or divisive. I was just in love. How do you put a lid on that?

and his purple Kool-Aid suicide drinkers, and I thought this sounded awfully similar. I honestly thought it was a cult. A plan began to form in my mind—a covert, special-ops mission. I decided to show up at this organization's discipleship school, go in undercover as a student and try to draw some of them to Christ.

With my last Army paycheck, I bought a Honda 400cc motorcycle, which I had no idea how to ride. I eventually learned, but not before crashing it so many times that I had knocked off all the pegs, mirrors and mufflers—you could hear me coming half a mile away. I roared up on that bike the first day of discipleship school dressed in the only clothes I had—my Army fatigues and combat boots. So much for keeping a low profile.

A bunch of people were milling around outside the school, and one woman approached me. She spoke English with what I later learned was a German accent, and she extended her arms to me in welcome. At that point in my life, the only way I categorized physical contact was either as aggression or as a sexual pass. Given my belief that she was a cult member, I jumped to the conclusion that she was also coming on to me. I was offended and angry, so as she threw her arms around me, I reacted. I plowed into her, knocking her to the ground.

I quickly realized that I had gotten the wrong idea when other people came over, helped us up and began trying to make friendly introductions. I met the leaders of the program, too, and despite my rather rough introduction, they decided to take me on as a student. Later they told me they had felt as though God wanted 68 people in their class. Until I showed up, they had only had 67, so they figured I was number 68.

My discipleship class consisted mostly of kids from nice, middle-class Christian families. I stuck out like a sore thumb with my Army attire and defensive, suspicious attitude. I did not speak the Christian lingo, and I maintained a general hostility that kept most of the other students at a safe distance. I even refused to sleep in the dorms with the other girls. (I did not know what they would do to me! Again, I was wary of either violence or sexual harassment—but the issue was all in my mind, not in any of their behaviors.) I sold my bike, bought an old car and slept there instead. I also refused to attend the "flock group" to which they assigned me. I had just come from an Army platoon, and now I was supposed to be in a girly flock group? *I don't think so*, I decided. I did not mesh with the girls I was assigned to do kitchen chores with either, so they soon sent me to work alone outside, cleaning up the property.

So much for the impression I was making as an undercover evangelist! As you might have guessed, the real impression was the one being made on me. Right from the beginning, the teaching was revolutionary for me. Our first teacher's first lecture was called "Pride, the Root of All Evil." I was coming from the Army, which had trained me that taking pride in ourselves was our chief virtue, so this pursuit of humility struck me as totally weak. The only problem was that the teacher had so much Scripture to back up what she was saying. I was still new to the Bible and to its authority as the Word of God, so after the lecture I went out in a nearby field alone and looked up all the verses she had taught about. They were all there, plain as could be. With each one, my heart began to break. I finally just lay on the ground in the mud, repenting for my pride.

It only took about two weeks before I began to seriously question whether I had been wrong about these people. Maybe this was not a cult after all, but the real thing. Maybe I was not there to convert them, but to learn from them. And maybe I had a lot more to learn than I had ever imagined. It certainly seemed that way. During the first three weeks of the program, many times I could not even make it through the teacher's Bible studies. As she laid out the basic truths of discipleship, like the fear of the Lord and becoming servants like Christ, the servant of all, God simply pulverized my heart. But because I was unwilling to show weakness by crying in front of the class, I would just get up and leave the room.

A few weeks into the program, the leaders met with me to see whether I was going to stick with it and pay the tuition, which I had not done. I could tell that some of them had doubts about whether I really belonged, but one of the leaders in particular pleaded with me to stay. This leader expressed such love and acceptance of me—even though I was so troublesome—that I could not help but be moved. In the end, I went out in the field, asked God what to do and heard Him say that He wanted me to stay. I came back, paid the tuition, moved into the dorms and began to fully engage in the training. Thirty years later, I still vividly remember so many of the lessons I learned and the experiences I had there. That program laid an invaluable foundation of the truths of the Gospel in my mind and heart.

### Alone in the Woods

I might have pursued further opportunities with that organization if I had not experienced a major disappointment soon after the discipleship school ended. Two of my leaders who had taught a class on morality ended up confessing to having an affair with each other. It devastated me. I had not yet gone far enough in my journey with Jesus to view such a choice with mercy and understanding, so I turned to my old friend anger to respond. I decided that Christians were all hypocrites, that I was done with them and that it was going to be "just me and Jesus" from there on out.

I moved up to Weaverville, a tiny town nestled in the beautiful Trinity Alps of Northern California. At the time, one of my brothers was serving a jail sentence in Weaverville. I thought I would just go find a secluded spot to camp nearby, read my Bible and visit him on visiting days. Thus began my season as a hermit living in the Shasta-Trinity National Forest. I had a tent, but I never lit a fire because I did not want to attract the forest rangers. All I did was pray and read my Bible. Once a week I walked to Weaverville, visited my brother and picked up some supplies with the Army stipend I still received.

As you can imagine, all that isolation started to get to me. But being stubborn, I probably would have stayed out there, getting crazier and crazier, if the Lord had not intervened. One cold winter night, I was caught in a freezing rain as I hiked to town. I took refuge in the general store for a bit, and I could see that it would be unwise to try to head back to my campsite. Once out there, I had no way to dry off and get warm. I had seen a little church across the street, so I headed over, found it open and empty, and decided to stay the night.

A couple of hours later, I heard someone come into the church. I quickly ran into the girl's bathroom to hide, hoping the person was a man. The bathroom was right by the sanctuary, so I could clearly hear this man come in, sit down at the piano and begin to play and sing beautiful, spontaneous worship. After a while, he began to pray for the congregation. There was no audience, no one for him to impress but Jesus.

I began to think, *Wow, this guy knows the Lord. Maybe there's another real Christian after all.* My heart suddenly became aware of its hunger—I had been in the woods for a long time, with no fellowship and no one to restore my hope in people. I would learn later that this man was named Bill Johnson, and that he was then the pastor of Calvary Chapel (now called Mountain Chapel).

I came back the next night and hid in the church bathroom. Sure enough, as I had hoped, Bill showed up again to have his time with the Lord. (I learned that this was his nightly routine after he tucked his family in bed at the parsonage.) My hunger and curiosity were growing by the minute, so I picked up a bulletin to see what else was going on at this church. I saw that there was an elders' meeting coming up the next night. Once again I decided to come back, hide in the bathroom and eavesdrop on the meeting. The "elders" turned out to be five or six guys in their twenties. Before they did anything, they worshiped. Then they discussed some church business, and then they prayed. I could hear them beating the ground, crying out for a move of God in Weaverville. My list of "real Christians" began to grow again.

I wanted to get closer to this group, but I was not ready to attend a church service. I looked again at the bulletin, saw they had home groups and picked one to try. It was hosted by Kris Vallotton, and I still remember walking out to his house that first night. I had no flashlight, and it was so dark that I had to walk along the yellow line in the middle of the road by moonlight. I can only imagine the impression I made, given my lack of social skills and human contact, combined with my long, unkempt hair and no means to bathe.

When Kris gave the teaching he had prepared, I mercilessly challenged him up and down on his use of Scripture (remember, all I did was read the Bible). I kept him up discussing interpretive questions long past the time everyone else had gone home. Poor Kris! But he graciously took me on, and our nights of vigorous conversation extended into months. Often Kris would finally say, "Look, it's midnight. I'm going to bed. If you want to crash on the couch, go ahead."

If I wanted to finish debating a particular point, I got up the next morning and followed Kris to his job at an auto repair shop. He would be on a creeper under a car while I sat beside him and argued over Bible verses. Over time, Kris and his wife, Kathy, broke through to me, forging a connection that has been one of the most significant of my life. The Vallottons' love and their faith in me did wonders to restore my faith in the Church, in people and in myself. Even more, they taught me how to be part of a family simply by bringing me into theirs.

Along with Kris and Kathy Vallotton, I have now been in relationship with Bill and Beni Johnson, Danny and Sheri Silk and Charlie and Julie Harper for over thirty years. We have never cut our wrists and exchanged blood, but there is a covenant relationship between us that has grown deeper through countless expressions of love and sacrifice. Throughout the years, these people have prayed me through near-death experiences, welcomed me into their homes and into the lives of their children, supported me financially, given me invaluable wisdom and guidance and otherwise shared the highs and lows of decades with me. There is nothing put down in writing, but we know we could ask each other for anything. This very book you are reading is a fruit of those covenant relationships.

## Danny the Dealer

As my heart toward the Body of Christ was restored through my new friends and family at Mountain Chapel, my heart to reach the lost and brokenhearted regained its passion as well. I spent a lot of time hanging out on Weaverville's Main Street, looking for people to talk to about Jesus. I quickly discovered that Weaverville had a thriving drug trade; the surrounding woods provided an ideal place to cultivate marijuana. "Mushrooms," LSD and other hallucinogens were also readily available, particularly during the summer, when teenagers and transients would cruise Main Street looking for action at its bars. I hung out between two bars there and talked with anyone and everyone.

One night, just as I was about to pray for a couple of street girls, another girl drove up to tell them there was a party at Danny's, the new drug dealer in town. By that point, I had heard about Danny and he had heard about me. I was the "Jesus freak" who was trying to steal his customers. I jumped in the truck along with the girls, planning to go to the party and meet him. The driver told me to get out, but I refused to do so unless she told me where Danny lived. She broke down and told me, so I climbed out of the truck and began working on a plan to meet Danny for a little chat.

Some days later, after hunting around, I found Danny's beaten-up shack on the edge of town. The window next to the door was broken, so I reached in, unlocked the door and stepped into what proved to be your typical drug dive—a filthy room furnished with a lone chair. Nobody was home, so I just sat down and waited.

Danny arrived at the house a couple of hours before dawn. After he closed the door, I said, "Hi, Danny." His surprise quickly turned into serious annoyance when I introduced myself as his competitor in Weaverville—the "Jesus freak who hangs out on Main Street."

Danny threatened to call the police and report me for trespassing. I advised him to do just that since I also wanted to talk to them about his drug dealings. Grudgingly, he suggested we call a temporary truce and work out our differences.

"Fair enough," I replied.

We talked for two hours. Danny, who was only 23 years old, told me that his single mom had provided him with a good upbringing, but he had derailed in high school, experimenting with marijuana and other drugs in his quest to fit in. Before he knew it, he was addicted and began dealing to support his habit. As our conversation went on, Danny began to pour out his pain. His life was full of insecurity rooted in being fatherless. Danny did not know who he was. The drugs anesthetized his feelings of inadequacy, if only for a moment. As a dealer he felt significant among his peers, but deep down he knew it was a sham. He finally admitted to me that he wanted out.

As the sun dawned on that dingy mountain shack, I told Danny about God's purpose for his life. To my joy, he embraced it wholeheartedly, repented and received God's forgiveness. He ended up making a total break from his prior life, leaving Weaverville and joining Teen Challenge, a Christian drug rehab program.

## The Amazon Woman

Danny was one of several drug users I led to the Lord in Weaverville. Unfortunately, some of them did not break totally free from their addictions or from the pull of their old friends. Ultimately, those users returned to their old bondages, which was tough for me to watch, but it made it clear that a lot more was going on in their lives than I could see on the surface. My eyes became increasingly open to the spiritual forces battling over their lives.

I will never forget one woman whom Kris and I reached out to; she was known around town as the "Amazon woman." Our experience with her taught us more about the reality of the "dark side" than I had ever understood up to that point. This lady was about six feet tall, wore a hairy bearskin coat and had long, dark hair with two curling, bleached locks at her temples that made her appear to have horns. She lived in the auto junkyard, and everyone knew she was crazy—the best word people had for *demon-possessed* in those days.

The Amazon woman had a habit of going to local bars and getting into wild fights—fights she usually won. At the time I was working as a nurse's aide in the Weaverville county hospital, and on several occasions a whole group of men showed up at the emergency room, all badly beaten up by this woman. The whole town was afraid of her. As you can imagine, word spreads like wildfire in small towns, especially horror stories. I did not believe all the uproar going around about the Amazon woman, yet I could not deny the broken men I saw in that hospital. Clearly, she was a force to be reckoned with.

One night I had a dream. I saw a cave going into a mountain, and the cave descended all the way into hell. God told me to go into the cave because He wanted me to bring someone out. As I journeyed deeper and deeper, I came upon different caverns that were home to different demonic strongholds. The Lord taught me how to take authority over each of them. Finally, I came upon a woman. Though I had not yet met her in real life, I knew it was the Amazon woman, and I knew that I was to bring her out and help her get free of these different strongholds. In the dream, she agreed to come with me. When we finally emerged from the cave, she began rejoicing in the light. But after two days of walking in the light, she turned around and walked right back into the cave.

Then next morning, I told Kris about the dream and we began praying together for this woman. Just a few days later, she showed up in our emergency room. In those days, we had no staff in the emergency room at night. If someone came, they would ring a buzzer and we would take the elevator downstairs, find out what the problem was and notify the on-call doctor. When the buzzer rang that night, a nurse and I took the elevator down together. As the doors parted, we saw the Amazon woman, who had kicked in the glass emergency room doors, standing bloody in a pile of glass and making strange growling noises. I hesitantly stepped forward, only to hear the elevator doors close behind me as the nurse took off, leaving me to face this lady all alone.

I froze, unsure of my next move. This huge, fearsome woman was snarling at me, obviously volatile. All I could think was that she was going to tear apart the emergency room and that I was going to get in trouble for it. I charged at her, tackled her to the ground, grabbed her hair and put her in a hold. As I held her, visions of the men she had beaten up flashed before me. *She's going to tear my arms off*, I thought. *She's going to kill me.*

To my surprise, instead of fighting back, she started crying. *Oh no*, I thought, *now I really am in trouble. I just assaulted a patient. What was I thinking?* I was confused, but also still too afraid to let go.

The Amazon woman started moaning desperately. "I'll do anything to get free. I'll do anything!" she cried.

I asked her what had happened.

"Two men came after me," she said. She explained that she had been running away from them in the dark and had tripped over some stuff in the junkyard where she lived, cutting herself up.

"Who were these men?" I asked her.

She began crying again, in obvious distress. Through her sobs, she admitted, "They're not men. They're demons."

She explained that she had been involved in what sounded to me like satanic ritual abuse while growing up in the San Francisco Bay area. She got scared and ran away to the mountains, but the demons followed her. Again, she repeated that she would do anything to get free.

I knew this was my moment. I took a deep breath and launched into the Gospel. At the name of Jesus, she went wild, flailing and roaring. Thankfully, the nurse who left me had returned, along with some men she had called to help. They rushed to help me restrain the Amazon woman and gave her a shot of thorazine to sedate her. After she was out, we put her on the table and stitched up her wounds. When she woke up, the doctor ordered that she be held for 72 hours in the "rubber room" for psychiatric evaluation.

Every patient in the rubber room needs their vital signs checked every fifteen minutes. No one wanted to check in on the Amazon woman, so although I was still quite scared of her, I went ahead and volunteered. I also called Kris and said, "Hey, the Amazon woman is here at the hospital. Can you come and speak to her? I'll get you in."

Kris came and met with her. He ended up leading her to the Lord. After the 72-hour hold was up, he took her home with him. I sometimes stayed with the Vallottons in those days, and given the circumstances and my dream about leading this woman to freedom, I wanted to stick around and help her. I shared the Vallottons' living room with this woman for two months. Though she still made us all pretty nervous, we started to see God powerfully at work in her life.

In one of our conversations, I told the Amazon woman my dream about her coming out of the hellish cave, but I never told her the ending. I was praying and hoping that she would not go back into the darkness. For those two months, apart from a few colorful incidents, she did pretty well and seemed to be enjoying her newfound freedom. But at the end of them, an old boyfriend of hers got out of prison and came for her. Though we pleaded with her not to leave, she went back to him and back to her old life. It was heartbreaking to see her make that choice, but in the end we just had to commit her destiny to the Lord and trust that her story was not over, even if our part in it was. The Lord had rescued me in spite of myself, after all, and He is still in the business of rescue missions.

# 4

# Raw Obedience

One of the central themes that began to emerge in my early years in Weaverville was the importance of obedience, of listening to the Lord's voice at all costs and knowing that what happens in the end is not my responsibility. Rather, it is my responsibility to obey and to let Him take care of the details. As with any child growing up, the value of obedience was revealed to me as much through failure as through success—a fact that I am not ashamed to admit. I have found that many people do not extract the "nutrients" from their failures because they feel ashamed of them, but God does not feel the same way. He is not ashamed when His kids stumble. He is right there to pick us back up, comfort us and teach us invaluable lessons about how to do better the next time around.

I learned one such invaluable lesson while working at that county hospital in Weaverville. When I got the nurse's aide job there, I could not wait to share the news of God's love with the sick and dying. Unfortunately, I quickly encountered a major obstacle to my fledgling ministry in the form of my nursing supervisor, Ms. Grimshaw (not her real name). Nurse Grimshaw's disposition was thoroughly intimidating—something like a cross between a Rottweiler and an overloaded Mac truck. To make matters worse, she was loud, pushy, built like a Sherman tank—and decidedly anti-Christian. She gave me a stern reprimand every time she caught me talking to my patients about God.

At first her intimidation did not deter me—it just made me sneakier. I would wait until I was privately bathing or toileting patients before telling them about Jesus. But it turned out that Nurse Grimshaw was sneakier still. She eventually caught me again and threatened to have me fired if I persisted in my "religious absurdities." That scared the heck out of me. I knew there were laws that banned Christians from praying in public schools, and I thought it was quite possible that Ms. Grimshaw had the authority to fire me if I spoke about Jesus in the county hospital. Jobs were difficult to come by in that small town, so for the sake of my job, I stopped sharing Jesus with my patients.

I worked the midnight shift, and a few nights after my last confrontation with Nurse Grimshaw, the emergency room buzzer rang. I scrambled downstairs to let the patient in. It turned out to be a couple coming from a party where the husband had begun to experience some mild chest pain. His wife had insisted that he go to the hospital. Nurse Grimshaw left him in my care while she went upstairs to notify the on-call physician.

I had about ten minutes to tell this man about the Lord before the Sherman tank returned with the doctor. I felt pressed with urgency to do that, but I was scared to death that she would catch me and have me fired. So instead of telling him about the Lord, I took his medical history. He was 39 years old and had no history of heart trouble. All he had was a dull, nagging pain in his chest and left shoulder. The urgency to share my faith with him intensified, yet I refused to listen.

Soon Nurse Grimshaw returned with the doctor. I moved to the back side of the gurney to make room for them. Suddenly, the man slipped into cardiac arrest and fell back into my arms! The three of us quickly swung his body onto the gurney and grabbed the crash cart. We hit him repeatedly with the paddles and did everything to resuscitate him, but despite our best efforts, he was gone!

After my shift, I slogged my way home through the snow in shock, tears stinging my cheeks. I felt utterly defeated. I had refused that man his last chance to hear the Gospel. Instead of obeying the Lord, I had succumbed to the fear of man. My head was spinning as the consequences of my inaction pressed deep into my soul, nearly tearing me apart. But from the ashes of my disobedience, I gained a new resolve. I determined that from that day on, I would never let the fear of man control my life again, even if it cost me my job—or my life.

A couple of weeks after that crisis, the Lord tested my resolve. He asked me to give up the job I had been so afraid of losing and move to Los Angeles to work in a Youth With A Mission (YWAM) crisis shelter for prostitutes, drug addicts and the homeless. I hated L.A., and I did not want to leave Weaverville.

I decided to take a drive up into the woods to argue with God about the move. It was winter at the time, and snow was piled high along the roads. Before too long in my conversation with God, my blood was starting to boil, and in anger I slammed my foot on the gas and drove my car straight into a deep snowbank. "I'd rather sit here stuck in a snowbank than go back!" I told Him.

Oddly enough, when I tried to back out, I found that I really *was* stuck. But I had given God my ultimatum, and I was going to stand by it. *Surely someone will come by soon and help me*, I thought. *Otherwise I can just hike out of here.*

Not a soul came up that road for three days. I spent the whole time pouting and complaining to the Lord. Finally, cold, hungry and realizing that I had become too weak to hike back to town, I got over myself and repented. I told God that I would go to L.A. even if it meant giving up my job, going back to the city where I had grown up (which, as you will see shortly, entailed dealing with some difficult issues of the past) and opening my heart to street people. Then I started praying for rescue! Thankfully, a little later a utility truck came up the road and pulled my car out of the snow.

## A Good Father

By the time He called me back to L.A., the Lord had already done much to redefine the word *obedience* for me. My experiences growing up and in the military taught me that obedience usually involved authority figures sternly demanding that I surrender my will to theirs, usually under threat of punishment. It was all too natural for me to project this paradigm onto God at first. This distorted view of God caused me to see the Gospel as a kind of "good cop, bad cop" scenario in which God, as an angry Father, would have preferred to wipe out humanity, but relented when Jesus talked Him out of it on the cross. While I was grateful that Jesus rescued me from hell, I was also too intimidated to draw close to that kind of Father.

Thankfully, God blew up the "punishing" paradigm for me through a powerful revelation of the cross He gave me while I was in the discipleship school. This revelation came to me in the midst of an internal conflict that had been intensifying with each passing day. I had a growing hunger to know God, but a sense of conviction for my sin was also increasing. The more I wanted to know Him, the farther away I felt. My soul was at war. I finally decided to fast and pray that God would give me a deeper revelation of the cross. I was a young Christian, so I really had no idea what I was doing, but I was so desperate for a breakthrough that I was willing to do anything.

One day while sitting in a rather boring class on biblical finances, I suddenly had an open vision of Jesus on the cross. I was shocked. I had had no idea of how horrific crucifixion actually was. Jesus was hanging there, absolutely shredded from head to foot and covered in blood. My first instinct was to look away, but I could not escape it. As I looked upon His mangled face, our eyes met . . . and I felt an acceptance and love so intense that my mind could not logically comprehend it. His eyes were like seas of passion inviting me deep into intimacy with Him. I was completely overcome by the realization that His desire for me was the motivation for His sacrifice. He was the one warring against the sin in me, because it diluted my affection for Him and separated me from experiencing His incredible love.

Before I had that vision, I knew sin was wrong, but I had no idea how much power it had to affect my relationship with God. I realized I had been minimizing my sin by comparing it to the sins of others. I had been thinking, *Well, at least I've never done anything as bad as so-and-so.* But in that encounter, I was completely undone by the revelation that God's judgment against sin was purely motivated by His incredible love for me. Jesus willingly bore separation from the Father and all its consequences—the physical pain, the emotional shame and the spiritual bondage—so that He could destroy my sin and the sins of the world once and for all. His love and sacrifice bore my sins away.

## Being Trusted

The cross forever removed the issue of punishment from the Christian life. The real issue is trust and obedience. When God told me to minister to that man in the hospital, and when He called me back to L.A. shortly afterward, He was asking me to trust Him and His Word above human threats or personal fears. What I did not fully understand then, but eventually came to recognize, is that faith is not one-sided. God was asking me to trust Him because *He trusted me* and wanted to trust me more. George MacDonald, one of my favorite writers on obedience, expressed this truth in a poem:

> We must do the thing we must
> Before the thing we may;
> We are unfit for any trust
> Till we can and do obey.[1]

MacDonald also said, "There are good things God must delay giving us. God must first make His child fit to receive and fit to have."[2] I think of a father who would love nothing better than to give his sixteen-year-old son a car for his birthday. But his son needs to learn to drive, prove that he can obey the rules of the road and demonstrate that he is trustworthy before his dad will even consider getting him a car. On the other hand, if the son is rebellious, lazy or cannot

1. George MacDonald, *Poetical Works of George MacDonald* (London: Chatto and Windus, 1893), 2:174.
2. George MacDonald, *Unspoken Sermons Second Series* (London: Longmans, Green & Co., 1889). Quote found at http://www.ccel.org/ccel/macdonald/unspoken3 .ix.html.

be trusted, then the father knows that giving his son a car will mean the young man's demise!

Though it will be different for each of us, what is the "car" that God wants to entrust to you or me? Jesus said, "It is your Father's good pleasure to give you the kingdom" (Luke 12:32). Our Dad wants to give us the entire Kingdom! The process of learning obedience makes us trustworthy to receive the prize of our Father's purposes for us.

I now understand that the depth of my obedience determines the level of authority I carry in God. In other words, the level of authority I have in the Kingdom is in direct proportion to my ability to submit to the King. This was the truth the Roman centurion recognized about Jesus—he knew Jesus had God's authority because He was *under* God's authority, fully obedient to God's marching orders. And the centurion recognized this because he also was "a man under authority" (Matthew 8:9).

It makes perfect sense to me that a military man was the one who recognized that Jesus' power signaled His submission to authority. The Army drilled a high value for obedience into my life. At first, all the orders and threats seemed extreme, but I realized later that soldiers entrusted with deadly weapons and commissioned to protect the nation must carry a profound sense of responsibility and authority. Likewise, the Father trusted Jesus to carry heaven's full arsenal and wealth with Him wherever He went because Jesus' heart was fully bound to His Father's will.

I appreciate Bill Johnson's perspective on what it meant for Jesus to walk around with unlimited power to raise the dead, kick out demons, cleanse lepers and heal the sick. Bill invites us to imagine what it would be like to wake up one morning and be able to cure just one disease with a 100 percent success rate—say, cancer. As soon as the word got out, our homes would be besieged by an unending line of desperate people willing to wait night and day for us to touch their bodies. If they had their way, we would never have time to eat, sleep or do anything but lay hands on them. In order to survive, we would have to turn people down, which would mean living with the knowledge that we were withholding their healing from them, at least for a while. Both our desire to help and the overwhelming size of the need could destroy us very quickly.

I have worked with the poor in developing countries for long enough that I understand well the stress of looking out my door and seeing an endless sea of people begging me to meet their physical needs. No one called to serve the poor will last long without developing healthy boundaries to protect himself or herself emotionally, psychologically and physically. These boundaries are only developed by listening to God rather than fearing the opinions of man. There are always enough time and resources to do what *God* has called us to accomplish. The only way my missionary colleagues and I could ever be trusted with growing numbers of church plants to develop, school students to teach, infants to feed and prisoners to love in a nation of extremely limited resources is that we have learned how to stick to the "orders from headquarters." We know that obedience is our only hope of survival. The moment we begin to rely on human agendas and prioritize human opinions above God's mandate is the moment we cut ourselves off from our source of authority, power and resources.

The relationship between obedience and covering—the place of safety, provision, rest and communion with God—is brilliantly depicted in Psalm 23 (NIV):

> The LORD is my shepherd, I lack nothing.
> He makes me lie down in green pastures,
> he leads me beside quiet waters,
> he refreshes my soul.

He guides me along the right paths
for his name's sake.
Even though I walk
through the darkest valley,
I will fear no evil,
for you are with me;
your rod and your staff,
they comfort me.

You prepare a table before me
in the presence of my enemies.
You anoint my head with oil;
my cup overflows.
Surely your goodness and love will follow me
all the days of my life,
and I will dwell in the house of the LORD
forever.

Of course, sometimes we do not feel very safe when He leads us through the shadows of death, where our enemies are waiting for us. When you find yourself facing the possibility of death at the hands of Communist guerillas, or bound in chains in a prison pit like Paul and Silas, or even in the fiery furnace like Meshach, Shadrach and Abednego, you initially do not think, *This is amazing. The Lord must have led me here!* You think, *God, where did You go? Did I do something wrong?*

Even Jesus, in His perfect obedience, cried, "My God, My God, why have You forsaken Me?" (Mark 15:34). But then you discover that it is in the dark valley that the God of the impossible shows up to protect you, break the prison chains, make you fireproof and even raise you from the dead. Nothing fuels your passion for trusting and obeying God like a walk through the dark. It is in this deserted place that the

Lord prepares a table for you overflowing with supernatural abundance, power, peace and protection.

## The Key to Knowing His Voice

It is important for us to remember that God does not live in the Bible, and that obeying Him does not simply mean following the Ten Commandments. It means walking in unbroken loyalty to His voice. Jesus modeled this remarkably for us. He resisted every force that attempted to knock Him out from under the covering of His Father's authority and get Him to do His own thing. He simply refused to be distracted by the voices of others. When the devil shouted at Him, "Worship me!" He told the devil to get lost. When the religious leaders tried to intimidate Him into submission, He instead healed another person on the Sabbath day. When the crowds or His closest friends and family members tried to control His divine agenda, He rebuked them. He even refused to listen to the voice of His own soul when it cried out in anguish in Gethsemane. Radical? Maybe, but obedience to God's voice is the key to unlocking the door to the impossible.

The idea that our lives are supposed to be directed by the voice of God scares the heck out of many believers. (And of course, the world thinks we are nuts when we tell them that we "talk to God.") Christians often ask, "How will I know if it's Him? What if I'm deceived? What do I do if He tells me to do something radical?"

Entire books have been written about how to discern God's voice, but I think we can gain the most insight into this just by watching mothers deal with their children. Have you ever noticed that mothers seem to have supersonic hearing? A mother can hear her child's cry in the midst of a noisy crowd of people, in another room or even at great distances. Mothers also seem to have some kind of heat-seeking, radar vision that can pierce through obstacles and recognize the slightest nuance of change in a child's expression. But the most impressive mom superpower is that "sixth sense" thing, where a mom just knows what is going on with her child.

You know what I am talking about. What gives a mother that uncanny, supernatural power of perception? I can tell you that it does not come from reading a book on motherhood. You do not get it from looking after someone else's kids, either. I think a mother's supersonic powers come from two things—her intense love (that "don't mess with my kid" love), and the constant, intimate interaction she has with her child.

I am learning that through intimacy with Jesus, I can develop a greater ability to discern His voice. I love what the author of the book of Hebrews said about believers: "Solid food is for the mature, who because of practice have their senses trained to discern good and evil" (Hebrews 5:14, NASB). Every one of us can train our "senses" to discern between the voice of God and the deceptive wranglings of the devil. Notice that we train our senses through practice, not by reading a book or trying to live vicariously through someone else's experiences. I have discovered that as I practice nurturing the presence of God in my life, like mothers nurture their babies, that "sixth sense" awakens in me and God's voice becomes very clear.

## Learning Obedience

Obviously, at times I have defiantly taken the long way around the mountain in learning to obey God's voice. Between experiences where I have failed—like in that hospital with the heart attack victim, then later ignoring the vision He gave me about leaving Oriental Mindoro before the guerillas invaded my village—I feel as though I have earned a Ph.D. in "what not to do" in the field of obedience. Mercifully, God has redeemed these experiences and used them to strengthen my loyalty to His voice and show me how faithful my Father is in giving me chances to try again. He trusts me not because I deserve it—after all, nothing in Christianity is about getting what we deserve—but because He cannot teach me to be a daughter without it. God's eternal perspectives help Him see past my most stubborn and ignorant moments (and believe me, I have had my share). God never has to "tolerate" us in our immaturity, because He sees the end from the beginning, and our end is glorious!

Our "what not to do" experiences are particularly valuable because they unlock the treasure hidden in one of the strangest verses in the Bible. Hebrews 5:8 (NASB) says, "Although He [Jesus] was a Son, He learned obedience from the things which He suffered." The idea that Jesus had to learn obedience is as mind-blowing as Luke's assertion that Jesus had to grow in favor with God (see Luke 2:52). But we find the reason that He had to grow in obedience just a few verses earlier:

> We don't have a high priest who is out of touch with our reality. He's been through weakness and testing, experienced it all—all but the sin. So let's walk right up to him and get what he is so ready to give. Take the mercy, accept the help.
>
> Hebrews 4:15–16, THE MESSAGE

Several years ago, I visited a refugee camp of about a thousand people who had escaped from Rwanda during the genocide in the mid-1990s. As many refugees do, these folks had taken on labels of rejection and abandonment. I heard many of them say things like "I'm forgotten," "I'm rejected" and "God has forsaken us."

I asked them, "Did you know that Jesus was a refugee in Africa?"

A few of them had Christian backgrounds. They said, "No, He was from Israel."

"Do you remember when Herod killed all the babies?" I countered. "The angel told Joseph to take Mary and Jesus out of the country, and where did they go?"

"Egypt," they said.

"And where is Egypt?" I asked.

"Africa!" they replied.

I could see the truth dawning on them: *Jesus was a refugee in Africa, just as I am. He knows exactly what it feels like to be pursued, hunted down, to be in hiding, to suffer the loss of his countrymen, his mother tongue. Maybe He hasn't forsaken us after all.*

This is why Christ learned obedience. He did it for us. He not only faced whatever we are facing; He was victorious. He aced every test so that He could turn around and give us the answers to all of life's questions. In all of life's challenges, we can be absolutely sure that He is there with us, happy to provide us with all the benefits of His victory. We just have to receive them.

### Giving Us His Heart

So what do you do when an intimidating Nurse Grimshaw comes along and exposes just how far your loyalty to the Father's voice goes? What do you do when you realize that your desire to please Him is not yet strong enough to resist the siren call of other desires? What do you do when the cost of obedience seems too dear to pay?

Let me first mention what not to do: be overwhelmed by guilt and shame. It never helps. Just admit that your love and trust need to be strengthened. Then invite Jesus to encounter you with His love and awaken your passion for Him. Invite Him to give you His very own heart to always do what "pleases the Father." I promise He will show up; He just cannot resist prayers like these.

I once had a dream in which I saw Jesus counting the cost to obey His Father. Jesus decided to give up all the joys of heaven—its majesty, glory and splendor. But above all, He gave up His Father's tangible love and affection. As He descended to earth, it got darker, hotter, stickier and stinkier, until He was born into a filthy feeding trough in Palestine. The dream continued by showing me snapshots of His life and ministry, each set in contrast to what He had left behind. Finally, I saw the horrors of the crucifixion and His descent into hell. At every point, I saw that from His vantage point, we were actually worth it. The dream ended with His ascending in victory over death, hell and the grave. The next moment, He was standing by my bedside. When I woke up, He was still there. I felt as if my body turned to jelly—because of the extravagance of His palpable love.

You were worth Jesus' obedience, and He is worth yours. He really did it all for you. His love for you is deeper and more personal than the most devoted mother for her baby; more than the most passionate lover for his beloved. When such love overtakes your life, it leaves no contenders. And the surest way to be overtaken by His love is to pursue His voice above all others.

# 5

# Back to the Streets

Despite the little obedience issue I had to deal with before I agreed to go work with YWAM in Los Angeles, I really did want to participate in what they were doing in their new crisis shelters there. I so wanted to be able to do more for people like Danny and the Amazon woman, people who needed help to start a new life after they embraced Christ. Bill Johnson and Kris both encouraged me to go; thus I found myself, for the first time in years, back on the streets where I had grown up.

I had not been working at the crisis shelters for very long before I found myself face-to-face with some old patterns of behavior that God wanted me to change. These patterns were the product of having grown up virtually fatherless due to my dad's long incarceration. We visited my dad in prison on weekends, but otherwise he was not present in my early life. My mother worked double time in a factory to support us, so my brothers and I were largely left to grandparents and baby-sitters. Living as we did in middle of L.A., we learned to settle most things with a fight-or-flight mentality. The only thing that mattered was who hit the hardest or ran the fastest. I learned from a young age to turn my fear into anger so that through violence I could protect myself.

Because I was dealing with street people at the crisis shelters, I immediately slipped my street-smart, protective instincts back on like comfortable old boxing gloves. One night at the prostitute shelter, I heard an alarming noise. I ran toward the noise just in time to see a man breaking into the house! He was a pimp who had come to get one of his prostitutes back. Instinctively, I did what was to me the most obvious thing in the world—I tackled him, fists flying. After a knock-down, drag-out fight that involved a tumble down the stairs, he finally took off running. I thought nothing of it—I never even questioned if my approach had been wrong. That was how you dealt with people on the streets.

After a few more such incidents, however, the YWAM leaders confronted me. "This is a problem," they said. "This is not the way to minister Christ's love and reconciliation to these people. We want you to keep working at the shelters, but we want you to first attend a three-month counseling course and gain some new skills for dealing with people."

### Forgiveness

I honestly did not see that I had such a big problem, but I wanted to stay, so I agreed to go through the counseling course the YWAM leaders suggested. My father issues were one of the first things it addressed. Up to that point, I had never really been upset that my dad had not been around. In fact, all my childhood friends had terrible fathers, so I actually thought I was lucky not to have one.

That mind-set quickly changed when the instructors began to teach us who God the Father is and who He intends our fathers to be in our lives. As I finally saw what had been stolen from me and how it had affected my life, strong feelings of anger and bitterness began to churn inside me. Then I heard the Lord say, "I want you to forgive your father." That put me over the edge. I left the counseling center and went to a small community church next door. I was livid, furious that God wanted me to forgive my dad when he should be the one asking for forgiveness. I began to vandalize the church in my rage, kicking down doors, punching out stained-glass windows, even pushing over the headstones in the graveyard. By the time my anger was spent, my hands were cut and covered with blood. Slowly, remorse began to wash over me as I realized that I had probably destroyed my chances of finishing the program and going back to the crisis shelters.

Meanwhile, another YWAM student arrived, saw my handiwork at the church and called the YWAM staff. Instead of judging me, lecturing me on self-control and sending me away as I had expected, they compassionately encouraged me to clean up my mess and work out my issues. They also contacted the church's pastor and explained my situation. The pastor was very gracious and understanding, and I paid for all the damages. One of the other YWAM students who was a doctor patched up my hands. I came back to class and sat through more teaching on the Father heart of God, through which I finally understood that the Lord wanted me to repent of my bitterness and forgive my father so He could heal me and help me receive His Father's love and blessing. As soon as I repented, I was bathed in an incredible sense of His overwhelming love, acceptance and forgiveness.

The final step in my healing process came when one of the instructors who had taught on the Father's heart came over to pray for me. During a break, he walked up behind me and put his hand on my shoulder. Instantly, my old protective instincts kicked in, and I turned and hit him. I was immediately devastated—I thought I had been healed of that angry retaliation. As I broke down, this man quietly got up, came over and began to pray for me. In my state of distress, I could not really put together all that he was saying, but I felt something change. Later, one of the staff told me that he had been breaking the spirit of violence off my life. From that point on, it was as though the thorn had been taken out of my paw. In an instant the violent, knee-jerk reactions and hypervigilance were all gone.

Proof that I really had been healed came when I returned to Los Angeles after the counseling course. My first day back in the shelter, a homeless woman who was having a really bad day came up to me and hit me in the face. I was surprised, but even more surprising was what I felt for her—there was no anger inside, only compassion for a broken woman. I could see that her rage had nothing to do with me; in fact, I saw that she was just like I used to be. Then she hit me again. That time, along with compassion, I felt incredible joy. I was healed. I was finally free. I almost wanted to say, "Hit me again!" just to feel the sheer exhilaration of that freedom.

## A Culture of Confession

God gave our YWAM team members a powerful key for both walking in freedom and leading people who were coming out of very broken lifestyles to walk in freedom. He led us to create a culture of gut honesty and accountability within our relationships. Every morning, the house staff met and openly shared whatever they were struggling with. People would admit, "I just wanted to get drunk yesterday," or "I was jealous of you," or "I was really struggling with lust last night."

Not only did this accountability help us guard our hearts since we lived in such a perverse culture; it also introduced those brand-new believers to the idea that "normal Christians" actually did confess to and pray for one another, just as the New Testament taught. Because we as a staff were already doing it with one another, it was very easy to turn to our street roommates or people at the breakfast table and ask, "Hey, how are you struggling? How can we pray for you?" They saw no pretense, no religious effort to appear holy and righteous. Instead, they saw what may be the central formula, if there is a formula, of the Bible: God gives grace to the humble, but He opposes the proud. We all need lots of grace!

This practice of mutual confession was not something mandated by YWAM; it was something we chose as a team because we saw that without a release valve for what we were dealing with on a daily basis, we would not last long. Our neighborhood was rough, to say the least. I could walk two blocks from my house to the men's house and count fifty prostitutes on the street, many of them selling drugs as well as their bodies. We had to have someone on duty in the houses around the clock. If you have ever worked with street people, you know that most of them do not sleep at night. Many are kicking their drug habits. After living for so long in such an unsafe environment, they have nightmares and other manifestations of fear. The stress involved in helping such people will make most anyone start looking for some comfort and relief pretty quickly. God has provided a Comforter for us, but if we do not plug in to Him, we will seek an illegitimate, counterfeit comfort somewhere else. As a staff, we fought to help one another stay plugged in to our true Source.

Of course, the payoff made it all worthwhile—the reward of seeing the real Gospel at work setting people free from bondages and addictions. I am not joking when I say that literally every day we saw people getting saved, healed and delivered. It was powerful.

I will never forget one of the prostitutes we helped. Over several months, I frequently saw her on the streets. A few times I handed her a business card with our crisis hotline number on it and invited her to call us when she wanted out. We had to let these girls find a safe moment to call us, because their pimps were watching them and would go to great lengths to keep them on the streets. Sometimes we got a call from a girl who said, "I'm at the [such-and-such] bar. My pimp is watching me, but I want out. Can you come and get me right now?"

If all went well, the girl would find a way to sneak outside and meet us safely, but sometimes her pimp would spot us and chase us through the city. Other times, as I have mentioned, pimps would break into the shelter house and forcibly try to take their girls back. Freedom was risky for these prostitutes, and often the girls would stay on the streets until something happened to make them desperate.

In the case of this particular girl, that desperate moment of decision came when her pimp decided, in a fit of rage, to beat her up with an iron. She called us from the emergency room. They had to shave her head in order to stitch up all her head wounds. I brought her home from the hospital and shared the Gospel with her, which she immediately accepted. The transformation in her life was dramatic. God freed her from anorexia and drug addiction, and she grew healthy and whole in every way. Wonderfully, she ended up marrying a pastor and going into full-time ministry.

I lost track of this girl after I moved out of Los Angeles, but five years later, when we both wound up doing a three-month ministry crash course in England, she ran up to me out of the blue and threw her arms around me. I hardly even recognized her. You would have never guessed that she was the same woman I had picked up from that emergency room. She was living, breathing proof that our Savior truly does make all things new.

## What I Live For

I am forever grateful that God led me in my early years with Him to places where, instead of being confused and trapped by powerless religion, I saw people set free and transformed by the real power of the Gospel. Those years established an unshakable confidence in me that what Jesus did on the cross was real and powerful—powerful enough to take the most broken, bound sinners and turn them into whole, righteous saints. Not only that, but I also came to understand that seeing such transformation was why I was on the planet.

I will never get tired of seeing souls who are caught in the web of sin and bondage encounter their Savior and find freedom. I will never get tired of seeing that incredible moment when they finally admit that the counterfeits and false comforts are robbing them blind, and they turn to the only One who can satisfy the deepest cries of their hearts. While I absolutely love miracles of healing and provision, my favorite miracle of all is the miracle of repentance. It is nothing less than supernatural when someone confesses his or her sin and receives Christ's forgiveness so completely that every bit of shame and guilt falls from him or her. It is resurrection from the inside out, and it is what I live for.

# 6

## Defying Death

As soon as the travel restriction I had inherited from the Army expired, I was itching to go overseas. Though I loved the fruit I was seeing at the shelters in Los Angeles, I longed to share the Gospel with people who had never heard it before. By that time, I had been certified as a medic and had also taken a tropical medicine course offered through YWAM. When the director of the course announced that YWAM was opening a clinic in the Philippines, I jumped at the chance to go. I sold my Honda and guitar, bought a one-way ticket to Manila and arrived with about two cents in my pocket.

Moving to the Philippines was an all-or-nothing venture for me. Though clearly I did not worry too much about being financially or culturally prepared, I did prepare myself for the big thing—death. I had heard all about the "ugly Americans" who were hated overseas. I naïvely thought that as soon we got off the plane and the Filipinos realized we were Americans, they might kill us, so my plan was to lead as many people to the Lord in the airport as I could before I entered the country. I know that sounds silly now, but that is what I thought back then. It was a wonderful surprise to learn that the Filipinos loved Americans. But it was also good that I had prepared my heart and mind for difficulties from the beginning, because in such impoverished and unstable countries, death tends to camp at one's doorstep.

This season of my life reminds me of a poem written by Christopher Logue:

> Come to the edge.
> We might fall.
> Come to the edge.
> It's too high!
> COME TO THE EDGE!
> And they came
> And he pushed
> And they flew.[1]

In the six years that I lived in the Philippines, I "came to the edge" again and again as I confronted death, disease, pain and loss as I never had before. And yet over and over, I found that the edge was exactly the point where Christ would begin to show His strength and love to me in unprecedented ways and lead me into the realm of the impossible. Along the way, I was forced to shed many of my ideas about Christianity, realizing that they were largely a mixture of spiritual philosophies, theories and religious American culture. But in their place, I began to discover the active, incarnate Gospel that transcends time, space, culture, economic status, gender and

1. Christopher Logue, "Come to the Edge" in *New Numbers* (London: Jonathan Cape, 1969), 65–66. Copyright © Christopher Logue, 1996. Used by permission.

age, and the One at the center of that Gospel, who leads us out of theory into reality itself.

## Smoky Mountain

The YWAM clinic where I ended up working for five years was established to serve the twenty thousand squatters who lived on a massive garbage dump outside Manila, right on the South China Sea. I was one of eleven medics sent out by the clinic to provide basic medical care to these souls.

My first reaction to the dump was to close my eyes and hold my breath. I did not even want the soles of my shoes to touch the ground. They called it Smoky Mountain because the garbage was continually smoldering in the oppressive tropical sun, and it would often burst into flames. Treacherous sinkholes filled with a scorching hot, tarlike slurry of composted refuse pooled everywhere, hidden under piles of windblown trash. Burning tires belched black smoke, creating a perpetual haze that hid the sun even on a sunny day. I never saw a single butterfly or flower on the dump. All you could see, through the smoke, were endless mounds of black and gray garbage, occasional fires, and barefoot squatters dressed in rags, digging with scavenging hooks for plastic, steel and other recyclable materials they could sell to a recycler. That was how they eked out their precarious living.

To make matters worse, high tides and storms regularly flooded portions of the dump, overwhelming pathways and shacks with a thigh-high tide of sewage, garbage, dead rats, dead dogs and even dead bodies. The stench was absolutely nauseating. Given these conditions, nearly everyone living on the dump was sick and had open wounds. The life expectancy was low. I lived there for four years before I saw anyone old enough to have gray hair, and that was a passing taxi driver who did not live on the dump. Beyond the squatters and smoldering pits, it was also a hideout for bands of criminals. The police never came near it, as they were outnumbered. The whole place was lethal—it was exactly how I had imagined hell!

My first day on the dump I went out to meet people, and a woman gave me something to eat. It was a gesture of friendship, and I had to accept it. Jesus did say, "Eat what is set before you" (Luke 10:8, NASB). As in most cultures, relationships there developed around shared meals, and Filipinos, being the generous souls that they are, frequently invited us to eat with them in their dump huts. Their delicacies included shish-kabobbed rats barbecued on an open fire fueled by garbage, fully fermented eggs with chicken embryos intact, "double-dead-dog" (a dog that was dead when they found it, which they skinned, cooked and ate anyway), gray worm burgers, boiled pigskin (bristly pig hair included), fermented fish head soup and fried guppy paddies with fish eyes and fins. Before the dump, I felt sorry for John the Baptist for eating locusts and wild honey. But now . . . I envied him!

I got violently ill with food poisoning from my first dump meal. I spent the night sitting on one bucket and puking into another. I had never been sick before in my life, and it was so bad that I thought, *This is it. I'm going to die on my first night.* I wanted to go home.

Then I heard the Lord speak to me: "Will you worship Me here, even though you're not in a comfortable, carpeted church with air-conditioning and padded seats?"

So I began to worship, stopping frequently to vomit and then continuing on in worship all through the night. By morning I was completely washed out, but I had a deep awareness of God's presence like never before. It was so wonderful that I felt I would rather be sick and know His presence than be well but unaware of Him. That encounter prepared me for the next twelve months, during which I was constantly sick with one disease or another. By grace, I stuck it out and began to serve, studied the Tagalog language, built relationships . . . and faced other dangers.

## Guns, Gangs and God

I was assigned to make home visits in a particular section of the dump, so I developed a regular route and got to know most everyone in the "neighborhood." One day, though not on medical duty, I decided to make the rounds just to visit people. Along the way, I came upon a group of eight men I had not seen before. I went up to them, held out my hand to shake theirs and introduced myself in my rudimentary Tagalog. They jumped up, startled out of what was probably a drug deal, and one of them put a gun in my face. I froze, hand still outstretched, knowing there was no escape. I could not run, duck or hide. He had me.

In that moment, a divine peace covered my body like warm honey. I knew it was going to be okay, though I also knew that death was staring me in the face. I did my best to explain who I was and why I was there, but I soon ran out of Tagalog words. And it really did not matter what I said—the gunman had made a move, and he intended to follow through with it, if only to avoid looking weak in front of his men.

I could see the anger in his face. *He's going to blow me away*, I thought. We both stood there for what seemed like an eternity, and then he sneered and pulled the trigger.

The gun did not go off. Astonished, the man looked at his gun and pulled the trigger again. But again, it misfired. It was as if God Himself had come down and disarmed the gun. After a moment, the man lowered the gun, came over and shook hands with me. One by one, all of his men followed suit. It was obvious to all of us that we had just experienced divine intervention, so I grabbed the moment and began telling them, as best I could in broken Tagalog, about Jesus. Providentially, someone came along who knew English and could interpret for me, so I was able to share the Gospel with them. After every one of those men had received the Lord, I went back to my base to get Bibles for them. When they found out I was one Bible short, they started fistfighting over them.

As I walked back to my place and processed this powerful, surreal turn of events, a strange feeling came over me. As usual, I had my eyes glued to the trail, watching out for glass and steel so I did not trip or cut myself. It then occurred to me, *Man, I could be walking the streets of gold right now, but here I am on this Asian garbage dump.* I knew I ought to feel grateful that I was alive, but part of me was depressed. In the end, I took it as a sign that God had protected me for a reason and that He would continue to provide what I needed to face what lay ahead.

### Learning Love in All the Hard Places

The emotional hazards of the dump were an even greater test for me than the physical ones. From the first day, God made it clear to me that my job was not to preach at the Filipinos, but to keep my mouth shut and learn to love—from them! This was a huge blow to my missionary pride and zeal, but it soon became obvious that what I thought I knew about love was mostly theory. I could quote the chapters and verses about love, but when it came to opening my heart to diseased, starving and dying people, my theories evaporated like a morning mist. And as always, the Lord was right—many of these "heathen," illiterate squatters knew a boatload more about love than I did. To this day I have never met such generous, hospitable, gracious, loving people. They would share their last meal with us foreigners and strangers, without regard for themselves. Their kindness was especially remarkable to me given the pervasive, continuous reality of their losses on every front.

After I had worked at the dump for about six months, an epidemic of measles swept through and killed about half of the children in the area where I was serving. We were burying them as fast as we could, while attending to the others in the hope of saving a few. It was so bad that we actually heard of another village that resorted to burying sick children alive in mass graves to stem the epidemic. I lost so many of my new friends, and I had no time to process the grief. The pain in my heart was suffocating, but being unable to escape this nightmare, I began to lock up and isolate myself emotionally. Eventually, I stopped pursuing relationships with the kids to cope with the fact that they were probably going to die. I grew terribly numb as my heart shut down.

One day I saw a child lying in the trash, left there by his family to die. He was bone-thin with starvation, and his head was deformed by hydrocephaly (water on the brain). This was one ugly kid. I knew we could not afford to treat him, and I had no intention of letting another sick child get close to my heart. But every day when I passed him on my rounds, I gave him some food and water. I was amazed each time to find him still alive. However, my heart was so numb that even though I passed him every day, I somehow could not allow myself to feel any love for him. I was that far gone.

Then one night, I had a dream about this boy. I dreamt that he died and was carried by angels to heaven. He was healed, whole, happy and absolutely beautiful. But for all eternity, he had no memory of anyone loving him on earth. I woke up sobbing, realizing that I was forfeiting an opportunity to impact this boy with God's love and create eternal memories for him. It was as if I had been shaken alive in the night. I immediately jumped up, hoping the boy was still breathing. Moving quickly, I knew I had to find my way back to his corner of the dump, dodging smoldering trash and potholes, before it was too late. To my relief, he was still alive. My heart raced with excitement for the first time in months, with this renewed sense of hope. As I took Rodrigo into my arms, I could feel the doors of my heart being pushed wide open again.

With some sticks for support and towels for padding, I propped Rodrigo up in a knapsack and started carrying him with me on my medical rounds. He was so malnourished that he hardly weighed anything. Before long, I was able to enroll him in YWAM's day-care program for kids on the dump, where he began to receive proper care—food, bathing and immunizations. (The program was able to expand, generally by one or two kids at a time, as more sponsors came on board to support that work.) Soon after, an amazing thing happened. God healed him! The fluid began to drain off his brain without any surgical procedure. In the meantime, we also found his family, who gladly received him back now that there was hope for his survival.

Rodrigo not only survived; he thrived. He quickly gained weight, grew hair and teeth, and soon learned to crawl and walk. He chattered, laughed up a storm and would often sing. There is really nothing more exhilarating than seeing a starving child come to life like that, something I have been privileged to see on many occasions since. I have seen totally emaciated, skeletal children on the threshold of death, fighting for the energy to breathe each breath, staring at me but too weak to cry. But if you simply put a nasal gastric tube in and start feeding them, after about a week they will turn a corner and start growing so rapidly that you can practically see them sprouting before your eyes. They can gain up to 10 percent of their body weight every week. They begin to make eye contact, become interactive and learn to play and talk. The joy that comes from saving lives like that—and saving souls—is what keeps you there, even when you are surrounded by death. Even the ones you do lose are eternally touched by the love you show them, even if it is simply to comfort them as they die.

Rodrigo taught me that we cannot pick and choose whom we will love and whom we will pass by. We must embrace all those the Lord brings us, just as He embraces us in our ugliness, disease, poverty and brokenness. If we are to learn to love as He does, we must be able to look beyond everything that has marred the person in front of us and see Jesus Himself. As Mother Teresa said of the poor she cared for in Calcutta, "Each one of them is Jesus in a distressing disguise." Seeing Jesus in Rodrigo, a son created in God's own image, was a supernatural gift that healed me and empowered me to be openhearted to others.

## The Valley of the Shadow

There was one particular season in the Philippines when I came to the end of my rope on every front. Everything was going wrong. I was completely broke. My parents back in the States were going through a divorce, and my family was in ruins. My heart was devastated by my ministry hero at the time, the internationally known Christian leader who had developed the tropical medicine course I had taken prior to going to the Philippines. This man moved to the Philippines with his wife and teenage children, but shortly thereafter, he ran off with a Filipino woman, abandoning his family on the dump with us. Watching him fall—a man who I thought was so much more spiritual than I was—rocked me. I thought, *What chance do I have of walking a life of purity or of maintaining a vibrant relationship with the Lord if he couldn't?*

To make matters worse, I had been sick for months. Beyond the continuous stream of gastrointestinal maladies, I contracted tuberculosis while treating the patients in a TB clinic I had started. I could not treat myself because I only had resources to treat the nineteen patients we had. I also had to hide my illness from the other medics because I was afraid I would be sent home. All I could do was secretly pray for my own healing.

I started sleeping in the coffin room so I would not keep my dormmates up all night with my violent coughing. The room was a reminder of the constant loss we lived with. We started building coffins and paying for burials as part of our ministry after we saw how traumatic it was for people on the dump to lay the dead to rest, a process that further compounded the already gruesome reality of death we saw almost on a daily basis. In order to pay the small fee for burial in a pauper's field, families often had to keep the body of a dead relative in their one-room huts for up to a month while they held gambling parties to raise the burial funds. Imagine having a loved one die and then having to live with the powerlessness and horror of having to keep the dead body in your rat-infested tropical hut made of trash until you could afford to bury the person.

Building simple coffins for people opened the door for us to do memorial services, which were wonderful opportunities for evangelism. Sleeping with the coffins, though? Not so wonderful. I felt completely alone. I had no cell phone or computer to help me get in touch with home; even snail mail was unreliable. I sent letters home asking for prayer, but I had no way of knowing if those letters arrived.

I had night sweats and lost a lot of weight. I knew I was slowly dying, but what I feared most was losing my faith. I could feel it slipping away. It felt as though I were hanging from a limb with my feet dangling over an enormous gulf of doubt. I wanted to hold on, but I simply did not have the strength or faith to do so. I was losing my grip on God and had no other place to turn.

## God, the Father of the Dump

Then one morning I got up, looked out the door of my shack and saw a man teaching his little daughter how to walk. He was holding her hands and guiding her steps over the uneven, dirty debris of the dump. At one point the little girl shook him off, wanting to walk by herself. He followed closely behind, hovering over her as she struggled to walk. Suddenly, she tripped. Right before she did a face-plant into the garbage, her father reached down and swooped her up. He had had her all the time!

God spoke powerfully to me through that experience. I knew in my heart that even if I lost my grip, my Father never would. I did not have to be afraid that I was not strong enough to hold on and keep it together—I was not, but He was. The book of Jude puts it this way:

> Now to Him who is able to keep you from stumbling, and to make you stand in the presence of His glory blameless with great joy, to the only God our Savior, through Jesus Christ our Lord, be glory, majesty, dominion and authority, before all time and now and forever. Amen.
>
> Jude 24–25, NASB

My attitude completely changed. As sick as I was, I began to press forward with confidence that my life was in my Father's hands. Shortly after this experience, I woke up one morning feeling different. For the first time in weeks, I could breathe deeply. I felt no urge to cough, and I felt so much stronger! I gave myself another PPD skin test, and miraculously the test came back negative. Normally if you have recovered from tuberculosis, the test will still be positive because it shows that your body has developed the antibodies to fight it. To this day, my body shows no evidence that I ever had TB. God healed me!

Needless to say, I was encouraged—though I had to keep the good news to myself because I had hidden the illness from the other staff. I later found out that one of the letters I had written asking for prayer had made it to my church, and the timing of their prayers and my healing coincided. That was also encouraging—more evidence that God, like the father of the little girl learning to walk on the dump, had had me all the time, holding me and keeping me.

It is so easy to refuse to "come to the edge" because of fear—fear of death, fear of pain, fear of loss. These fears are all too natural. But we must realize that fear will always betray and sabotage our ultimate purpose. It is in these dark times that we have to remind ourselves that our Father has taken hold of us and will not let go. Although your edge may not look like mine, God's promise to save us is the same. Maybe it is time to step out and learn to soar!

# 7

# Learning to Run

As I did with my street-smart hypervigilance and violence, many of us carry the hang-ups of an orphan heart into our relationship with God—ways of doing life that we often do not even realize are terribly broken until God graciously confronts us with a better way. Like a skilled physician, our Father also knows how much healing we can handle at any given time. Sometimes His timeline for restoration does not make sense to us. (You know what I am talking about if you have ever asked, "Really? Am I still dealing with this one?") But as long as we keep yielding to Him, we can be sure that He is healing and restoring us at the perfect pace.

Even as God heals us, however, it is vital to understand that He is not turning orphans simply into functional citizens, but into royal sons who look like Jesus. To use Paul's metaphor, in order to run the race of the Christian life, we must not simply be healed of our broken legs—we also must train them to run with speed and endurance. And everyone knows that in order to build speed and endurance, you must consistently push past convenience and comfort. Similarly, as we learn to run as sons and daughters, God will lead us to face challenges that are difficult not so much because of wounds in our past, but because they press us to our limits of faith, emotional and physical strength, social skills, knowledge and love.

One of the primary goals of this training is to help us align our desires and expectations with God's desires and expectations for us and let Him define our successes, failures and assignments. It is only by embracing our Father's goals and expectations that we run the race to win, for He designed the racecourse in the first place.

## The Journey into His Expectations

As you have seen, my years in the Philippines, which culminated in the extreme highs and lows of that year on Oriental Mindoro with which I began this book, were filled with experiences that tested and stretched me beyond my limits. Perhaps the greatest challenge of those years, though, the one that ended up doing the most to align my expectations with God's, was how that time in my life ended.

After my divinely orchestrated escape from the guerilla rebels in Oriental Mindoro, I hitchhiked back to Manila and went to the Department of Immigration to renew my visa, which had expired while I was trapped with the rebels. To my dismay, they rejected my renewal and gave me three days to leave the country.

My heart was torn; I was not ready to go back to the United States. Nothing felt good about leaving behind so many who had become my friends and family in the Philippines. In addition, a close missionary friend with whom I had worked there had vanished, and I desperately wanted to find her. (To this day, she has never been found.) Some friends helped me scrape together some money and flew me next door to Hong Kong, where I hoped to find a way to return to the Philippines. I stayed there for a few months, smuggling Bibles into China and teaching English to Chinese businessmen. But in the end, all my strategies for getting back to Manila failed. Once again I became desperately sick, this time from parasites. In my desperation, I cried out for help.

Dear friends from the United States flew me home. I underwent surgery, and my friends nursed me back to health. A dear couple, the Austins, encouraged and supported me as I pursued my physician assistant (PA) degree at Stanford University. They counseled me through my enormous struggle over being back in America. I am so grateful for their love and care at a time when I was dealing with pretty serious reverse culture shock.

On top of that, I was carrying a heavy burden of disappointment, confusion and guilt. Though God had been faithful to protect me in the Philippines and had helped me escape from the guerillas, I felt I had failed Him by not obeying Him when He first told me to leave the island. I also felt guilty for abandoning my Filipino family and my lost missionary friend. I had nightmares most nights.

In general, I was disappointed by how that chapter of my missionary career had ended—I had left too many things unraveled and unresolved. Though I continued to share the Gospel and was furthering my education so I would have better skills to take back to the mission field, I felt largely alienated from the American church and even from God. Inside, I was a mess of pain. Confusion had begun to run its course. I was living in my car again and barely getting by. At last, however, I graduated.

## Uzbekistan

After Stanford, I took the first job I could get overseas—I joined a team of Peace Corps workers in the newly formed country of Uzbekistan. Though the Soviet Union had collapsed, thanks to years of Communist propaganda, the culture was still deeply imprinted with hostility to Westerners. Many of the idealistic Peace Corps workers who had come with me were unprepared for how dangerous the country was; some sadly became victims of violence and rape.

One day I came out of my house, locked the gate and looked up the street to see my neighbor glaring at me. He had a massive guard dog standing beside him. Suddenly, without any provocation, the man sicced that beast on me. Instantly my heart dropped to my stomach; I only had a split second to respond before being mauled. Without thinking, I reached to the ground and grabbed a brick to throw at the dog. By the time I lifted up the brick, the dog was already in midair, jaws aimed for my throat. I shoved the brick right into his mouth and pushed him aside. We both staggered back and fell. He shook the brick from his jaws while I managed to grab another, preparing myself for round two.

Sure enough, the dog came at me again in full force. I slammed the second brick into his mouth, this time breaking teeth and tearing flesh from his gums. In the same fashion as before, we both fell aside. However, this time after pulling away, the wounded dog hesitated, looking to its master for the command. By this point I was pumping with adrenaline and anger, almost hoping he would try again. Instead, I looked at the man and said, "Three?" (The word is the same in Russian and English.) Sneering, the man called his wounded dog off.

I returned to my house and shook for thirty minutes as the adrenaline wore off. I cried, laughed, worshiped and cried again. That experience, and many others, made it obvious to me that God was not only with me, but was protecting me. Yet my heart also felt somewhat dry. I was having trouble really connecting with the Lord. Reading the Bible was like reading some kind of software code. The heavens had become brass. I could not hear Him, and I was almost positive He could not hear me—at least, that is how I felt. Night after night I went out alone in the Asian desert and wept, longing to feel His presence and the resolution my heart was seeking. It just would not come.

### What Happened to Weaverville?

After two years in Uzbekistan, I decided to return to Weaverville for a while to reconnect with friends, work and save some money. On the way home, I visited a friend in the United Kingdom who took me to a Christian music festival in Stoneleigh, England. This was when the Toronto Renewal had just broken out in the UK. It was the first taste of the renewal that I had seen. I can hardly describe how shocked I felt at the sight of ten thousand Brits camping in the rain, dancing wildly, laughing hysterically and joyfully rolling around in the mud. I had worked with many Brits overseas, and they had all been stoic, educated and never prone to extravagant displays of emotion.

At one point, an older woman in a purple frock waltzed by me, waving a scarf, and suddenly I heard the Lord speak to me clearly for the first time in five years. He said, "Do you see that old lady? She's a new wineskin. And you, young lady, are an old wineskin."

If I had been shocked before, now I was devastated. *This is what You want to say to me after all this silence?* I responded. But God had my full attention, and that is the way He wanted it.

I arrived in Weaverville to find more of the same frightening, intriguing madness going on in my home church that I had witnessed at Stoneleigh. All my friends from Mountain Chapel seemed to have eaten from the same tree as those Brits. After sitting through an uncomfortable Sunday service, I went to visit a good friend and church leader, Mary, to ask her what was going on. Within moments of talking with her, I was sure she was on some kind of upper drug—she was bouncing off the walls with excitement. She said, "Oh, I've got to show you this video of our women's retreat. It just changed my life. It set me free!"

I was curious, because I knew Mary had experienced many hard things in her past. But instead of seeing Bill Johnson giving a powerful teaching or prayer as I expected, all I saw on the video was a bunch of my friends on the lawn running around with flags, dancing and laughing hysterically. I finally got so freaked out that I said, "I need to run. I'll catch you later."

I jumped in my car and drove to another friend's house, but this friend was the same way—she was flying like a kite. I thought, *They're all possessed.* I was starting to feel scared and lost, like home was not home anymore.

I decided to give it one more shot before I packed up and left town, so I drove to my friend Jackie's house. Jackie immediately saw that I was struggling with what I was seeing, and she calmly invited me to sit down, have a cup of tea and talk. After some conversation, however, she dropped a bomb: "I've invited the Harpers and Kris over to pray for you," she said.

I immediately jumped up, grabbed my shoes and ran to the door, intending to hit the road for good. It was too late, though. Kris and the others met me at the door. After they came in, I said, "Look, guys, thanks for coming, but I don't believe in this stuff. I'm sure it is some kind of emotional hyper-spiritualism, or some conjured-up, humanistic need being filled in a really weird way. Whatever you say, it's not going to have any effect on me because I don't believe in it."

Kris said, "Well, let's do this—let's all sit for five minutes. We won't lay hands on you. We won't pray out loud. We'll just sit and wait on the Lord."

That sounded pretty safe to me. After all, except for that moment in England, God had not talked to me in years. I thought, *I'll sit for five minutes, say "See?" and leave.*

God can do a lot in five minutes. Before that time was up, I was lying on the carpet, tears and snot flowing, as God went right to the core of all the hurt, shame, regret and confusion I had carried all those years since I had come back from the Philippines. Gently, but with surgical precision, He exposed all the false guilt and shame I had taken on and just let them fall away, leaving me with a wonderful sense of clarity and peace.

I saw that I had never disappointed God, and what is more, that He had faithfully cared for me every step of the way. For the first time, I realized that I had never been responsible to carry my friends the way I had. It was as if God lifted off a massive weight that had been crushing me. It had been there for so long that I had accepted this burden as if it were part of me. However, God released me within moments from those years of bondage. When I got up, I knew I was healed.

### The Return of a Child's Heart

In the months following this encounter, I witnessed so much powerful fruit released through the outpouring of God's presence. People I had known for decades were getting free of addiction, bondage and illness, being reconciled with spouses and family members and living with freedom and joy such as they had never known. For me, one of the main themes of this season was learning to live in the freedom of being a daughter who, like Christ, was responsible simply to see and hear what the Father was doing and join Him at His invitation—no more, no less. I was not to be deceived into striving under false obligations and burdens. My responsibility was to enjoy intimacy with Him—recognizing that this is the source of greatest fruitfulness.

As I pursued this goal of intimacy and connection with God, I came into greater alignment with His purposes. I unlearned even more of my old, emotionally dishonest ways and stopped putting up protective walls when I felt vulnerable. I also learned to stop beating myself up when I was not successful. Instead, I quickly received His correction and tried again.

Incidentally, the ability to learn from failure is probably the greatest quality necessary to be a missionary. No scenario is really more filled with opportunities for faux pas than trying to live in another country, enter another culture, speak another language and serve another society. You are bound to get mud on your face on a regular basis! The sooner you take on a childlike attitude and fall in love with learning in all its messiness, the more at peace you will be.

The years of carrying disappointment had shut down a childlike heart in me, but God graciously restored that childlikeness—with a new resilience and depth. In the process, I discovered a paradox of spiritual maturity—we get younger as we get older. The more we possess the voracious curiosity of sons and daughters who embrace lessons in both success and failure, the freer we are to lead confidently as spiritual mothers and fathers who know that with Him, we ultimately cannot fail.

I have found that the spiritually mature look nothing like the world's typical adults who have lost their hope, dreams, passion and vision and are looking to finish their days in quiet retirement. Instead, like Caleb, whose faith kept him young and strong for 45 years even as his entire generation died around him in the desert, the spiritually mature know how to tap in to God's measureless, renewing strength so that they can complete their assignment in the earth and leave an inheritance for their sons and daughters. As Isaiah promised, those who wait on the One who "does not grow tired or weary" will "run and not grow weary" (Isaiah 40:28, 31, NIV).

# 8

## Wild Trust

One thing that has been true of my relationship with Christ in every season is that He loves to invite me to step out and take some outrageous leap of faith into the unknown with Him. I have become convinced that risk is God's love language. Like a father playing with a child, the Lord loves to throw me up in the air just to prove that He will always be there to catch me. Over the years, the risk-taking lifestyle has forged a firm foundation of confidence in my heart. No matter how impossible or unlikely the circumstances appear, when God asks me to jump, I do not have to wonder. I know His arms are waiting.

One of the more dramatic adventures the Lord led me on occurred in the early 1990s, when I was living and working on the island nation of Kiribati near the Marshall Islands. One day I heard Him say, "This time next year, go to the Syrian and Iraqi borders of Turkey." It was as clear as a bell. I did not know why; I just knew it was God. I had no clue what was going on in that part of the world. Even after a bit of research, it appeared that nothing much was happening beyond the region's usual unrest, except that a few disgruntled Kurds were being shuffled around those borders. Nonetheless, I began to pray daily for the region and plan a trip for the following year. After expressing my heart to a few friends, an intercessor friend from my church decided to join me on this escapade.

As the months ticked by, it was as though a bomb had been set, and it was only a matter of time before an explosion in the Gulf happened. The brewing conflict between Iraq and the United States intensified weekly. By the time my friend and I headed to Istanbul, the United States had given Saddam Hussein some ultimatums and had threatened war if he did not comply. The United States was planning to use Turkish airspace to launch a military campaign against Iraq, and to say the least, not everyone was happy about that. It definitely was not a popular time to be an American Christian woman in Muslim Turkey. To make matters worse, I did not blend in at all with the dress code for Muslim women (if you can imagine that). All I had were long johns (it was winter and bitterly cold), jeans and a bright blue parka. You could tell I was an American from a block away. So much for my covert mission!

Despite my requests for information about what I was to do or where I was to go on this trip, the Lord had kept me in the dark the entire year. I made the journey simply out of raw obedience. My only plan of action was to prayer-walk that border region, but even that seemed impossible, arriving as we did in the midst of a Turkish military deployment. I am not sure if you have ever tried prayer-walking through a military deployment zone—the military tends to frown on it. Our only option was to place the whole affair on the altar and trust. I began to pray, "Lord, I've come as far as I can. If You

want me in those border towns, You've got to make a way."
Meanwhile, all my friends thought I was nuts for making this
trip. They always think I am a little off my rocker anyway,
but they took care to express it more adamantly this time.

The day after we arrived, I tooled around Istanbul and
wandered into a bookstore. The proprietor, a young man by
the name of Zeki, happened to speak English, so I took the
opportunity to tell him about Jesus. It turned out that he was
already a believer. As our conversation continued, we began
to talk about the impending war. Zeki mentioned that he
was from a village on the border—the very one I had hoped
to visit. He had been unable to visit his family for two years
because of finances, but as you can imagine, he was desperate to see them before chaos broke out. Without hesitation,
I told him that I would pay for his flight if he took me and
acted as my interpreter. He agreed. I finally felt a sense of
breakthrough! At this point we decided that my intercessor
friend should remain in Istanbul to pray for our mission.

Two days later, Zeki and I boarded a plane to Diyarbakir.
All around us, the political situation continued to intensify.
The president of the United States had just declared war on
Iraq that day. As the plane approached the airport, I could
see chaos all around me. Thousands of Turkish soldiers were
being deployed in hopes of taming the sea of Kurds now in
full-blown riot.

The place was a ticking time bomb about to explode, and
we were landing smack-dab in the middle of it! The tension
was so heavy that I could feel it pressing down on me like a
wet blanket. Just as Zeki and I flew in, the airport was seized
by the government and turned into a military landing strip. We
had no idea how we were going to get out of the region, but
at the moment, that was the least of our concerns. In all the
mayhem, Zeki and I managed to find a bus that was heading

toward the border. He knew a safe place on the way where we could lie low and stay the night, a monastery where he had been sent as a boy to be trained as an Orthodox priest. Off we went!

When we arrived at the monastery, it felt as though we had gone back in time. It was an ancient place where monks had lived, prayed, studied and died for centuries. I had a strong sense that I might have been the only woman ever to grace their threshold! The monks were thrilled to see us (to see Zeki, anyway). They accommodated us for the night and agreed to provide us with transportation to his home village the next morning.

Zeki talked with me long into that first night about his personal heartache. He had never been able to finish his training and secure a position as a priest in a village. He had to be married to be a priest, and Christians suffered such persecution that most women did not want to be Christians. They especially did not want to be the wife of a priest. Zeki, therefore—a handsome, caring and godly man—ended up single, working in a bookstore in Istanbul. To make matters worse, his parents hundreds of miles away were on the brink of war. As I thought through his predicament, Zeki's story pressed heavily upon my heart. Talk about living a life of courage and sacrifice!

The next morning, we embarked on the journey to Zeki's house. All along the road, we encountered police and military roadblocks. Yet, despite my being a neon-blue-clad American woman with no head covering amidst a busload of black-clad, fully covered Islamic women, the soldiers inspecting the bus ignored me altogether. It was almost as if I was so obviously out of place that I was invisible to them. Eventually we made it past all the checkpoints and roadblocks. After a long journey through the rough roads of Turkey, we finally arrived at Zeki's home.

Just like at the monastery, I found myself in awe of Zeki's village. I was literally standing in the middle of biblical history. The villagers were descendants of Syrian shepherds who had migrated up into the border of Turkey through the ages. They still lived in stone houses and caves, and they raised sheep out on those rocky, desertlike plains. For generations they had been beaten down and slaughtered by Muslims venturing through their region. Many of them expressed to me their conviction that this latest conflict with Iraq would spell their final demise.

In spite of all this, Zeki's family and friends bravely welcomed me and took the time to introduce me to their ancient form of Christianity. We ventured deep into their ancient catacombs, where they traced their spiritual family roots from their current leaders all the way back to the apostle Paul. They showed me their prayer beads and the thick, handwritten Bibles they had copied and handed down from generation to generation. I saw walls pockmarked with bullet holes where Muslim radicals had gunned down their forefathers. It was all so amazing, and sad at the same time. I could not believe what I was seeing. Later on, they let me worship with them. In their worship, which was liturgical, the men stood facing each other in a square with the women around them. They chanted the service, much like a Gregorian chant. Their worship was very sincere and very deep—it was obvious that they knew the Lord and had a profound reverence for Him.

As I met with these simple believers, I was taken aback by the Lord's love for these people . . . that He would send me halfway around the world, through dangerous territory, just to pray and encourage them in their time of trouble. And it was quite a crowd I was able to connect with. Not even counting Zeki's friends, his "family" was more like a tribe—there were around 150 of them, and they comprised five generations.

To be honest, if the Lord had given me any more information about the escalating conflict and all the hazards involved, I probably would not have gone. I have come to realize that if I ask Him something and He does not answer me, there is often a good reason! The truth is that we do not need to know all the details. We just need to trust the Man who has the answers. The more we trust Him, the freer we are, regardless of the circumstances. Frankly, trusting Him makes life fun.

Do not get me wrong—I do not flippantly wander into dangerous situations or war zones just for kicks. I just know that when God speaks to me, He is going to fulfill His word. Everything about God is supernatural, so walking with Him inevitably launches us into a supernatural lifestyle. And I know that if I go where He sends me, it is always going to be okay, whether I live or whether I die. For to live is Christ and to die is gain!

## Trust

Have you ever wondered what it must have been like for the disciples when they first encountered Christ? Personally, I think it must have been a mixture of bizarre, confusing and irresistibly compelling. Jesus gave most of the disciples only a brief, perplexing invitation: "Follow Me" (Luke 5:27, NASB). Imagine going to a job interview, and instead of being asked questions or offered a salary package with benefits and stock options, you simply hear, "Come with me." Most of us would be pretty uncomfortable following someone into the unknown with so little explanation. Actually, I do not think anyone in their right mind would go.

That first step of faith became a lifestyle for the disciples. Jesus never really did a lot of clarifying; in fact, much of what He said was mystifying and created more questions than answers. The Gospels suggest that the disciples had little idea what the plan was from one day to the next, which is crazy. Imagine working for a boss who sent you on a business trip with no luggage, no food, no money, no hotel bookings and not even any scheduled business meetings. Do you know even one church today that would organize a mission trip the way that Jesus did? Yet the disciples and many others willingly followed this Man on this supernatural adventure. And it was not for any "package" He proposed to them, because the only thing He offered was Himself! Apparently, these men and women found Him compelling enough to leave their careers, families and other pursuits to follow Him (see Luke 5:11, 28).

In case you are wondering, Jesus is still in the business of making disciples, and He has not changed His leadership style one bit. The most challenging thing about following Christ is that His greatest concern is not for our comfort. Before we get to know Him, many of us wonder about Jesus' motives for leading us as He does. Does He enjoy scaring the heck out of us? Does He want us to remain ignorant slaves who blindly do as we are told? Far from it! In fact, He wants to give us comfort, understanding and many other amazing things that emerge out of an intimate relationship with Him. He is passionate to connect with us and reveal His intense glory to us, for as we get to know Him we become like Him. Yet deep, intimate relationships can only be built on the foundation of complete trust.

This is where the risk-taking and discomfort come in. Jesus so loves us that He wants us to trust Him more than anyone else or anything else. He is the ultimate expert at identifying our objects of trust, particularly the things we rely on to protect us from our greatest fears and to fulfill our deepest desires. Therefore, He is a master at confronting us with choices that encourage us to break our attachment with these things and put our trust in Him instead. If He allowed us to stay within our boundaries of fear, we would never reach our full potential in Christ.

It is scary to let go of tangibles to embrace the invisible. In my walk with the Lord, I have had to continually remind myself that when I let go of the world's security, I get to embrace Him and the supernatural. Thankfully, five times Jesus promises us abundant blessings for making this exchange. Here is Mark's version:

> Assuredly, I say to you, there is no one who has left house or brothers or sisters or father or mother or wife or children or lands, for My sake and the gospel's, who shall not receive a hundredfold now in this time—houses and brothers and sisters and mothers and children and lands, with persecutions—and in the age to come, eternal life.
>
> Mark 10:29–30

## Faith Like Gideon's

I love the story of Gideon because he was a man who took God at His outrageous word, exchanged the visible for the invisible and ended up doing the impossible. His story, like most God stories, begins in the midst of insurmountable odds. The Israelites, despite living in the Promised Land, were being so oppressed by the surrounding nations that they were making their shelters in caves and clefts of rock. Every year the Midianites and Hittites worked their way through Israel's land, decimating their people and crops and leaving them with nothing. If you ask me, that does not sound much like a land of promise! However, God heard Israel's cry and responded to it. He knew just the perfect man for the job . . .

God found His man threshing wheat in a winepress. In other words, Gideon was hiding, trying to keep his secret cache of food out of enemy hands. The guy was terrified, and I am sure he did not feel much better when the angel of the Lord showed up and talked to him as though he were someone important: "The LORD is with you, mighty warrior" (Judges 6:12, NIV).

Then again, maybe the angel was not all that intimidating, because Gideon felt free to express his doubts. (I am paraphrasing from here on, as you will see, but for the full story, read Judges 6 and 7.) Gideon basically said, "The Lord is with me, huh? I don't know. I really don't see the Lord with any of us these days. From where I stand, Israel is looking pretty abandoned. I mean, our parents told us all about God delivering them out of Egypt and about the miracles that happened, but where is He now? He's just letting our enemies take us out."

I love the Lord's response to Gideon. He was not offended; He had shown up for the sole purpose of answering Gideon's doubts. "Yeah, Gideon," the angel responded, "the stories are all true. But you forgot to mention an important detail. If you remember, God delivered your fathers out of Egypt by sending a man to lead them and to do My wonders. And guess what? This time, I'm sending *you*."

In classic Moses fashion, Gideon stammered, "Whoa, sorry, but I think you have the wrong guy. Save Israel? Shouldn't you be talking to one of the big tribes or clans? I'm the baby brother. No one's going to listen to me."

"Right," the Lord answered, "you're also forgetting that Moses was an outcast sheep farmer with a speech impediment when I sent him to Egypt. I like to work with weaklings. All you have to do is believe that I will be with you. And by the way, you're going to do awesome. When we're done, all the Midianites will be dead."

To make a really amazing story short, God sent Gideon to initiate Israel's deliverance by cleaning up their idolatrous mess. Gideon's first move was to tear down his father's altar to Baal and cut down the Asherah pole beside it. This, of course, started a family feud, but it ended with everyone rethinking Gideon's default status as the baby brother and giving him their respect and allegiance.

If you read the story through Gideon's eyes, however, you can feel the stress his first act of obedience put him under. He had just torn down the gods his family had hoped would save them, and now he had to prove that the real God was on his side and actually would save them. And Gideon did not have a lot of time. Israel's enemies were gathering to destroy their land and take their crops in a matter of days. Gideon had been put in the ultimate bind—the kind where God showing up is the only hope.

As the story goes on, God in all His love gave Gideon ongoing opportunities to pin all his hopes on Him, not on any human strategy or strength. Gideon initially gathered a massive army of thousands, but that was too many. God made him whittle it down to a mere three hundred brave men. Then He gave Gideon what might be the most ridiculous military plan in history. Gideon was to equip each of his men with a trumpet in one hand and a jar with a torch inside it in the other. No swords. No bows and arrows. No spears. No shields. Not one person in God's army was carrying a weapon! Then God commanded the three hundred men to space out and surround the massive enemy army. On Gideon's command, they marched to the edge of the camp, blew their trumpets and smashed their jars, shouting, "A sword for the Lord and for Gideon!" The sound released utter confusion and panic into the heart of the enemy. The Midianites turned on each other, slaying their own troops to the last man, just as God had promised.

Like Moses before him, Gideon found out that all he really needed to hear from God was, "I will be with you." An incredible bond of trust was formed between God and Gideon on the battlefield of self-abandonment. Through Gideon's courageous choices and unyielding obedience, the impossible happened—a nation stepped back into its rightful place with God, and the people's inheritance was restored to them.

Those five words, *I will be with you*, are our security when God invites us to face an impossible circumstance. When we trust His promise to be with us, not only will we find ourselves doing the impossible; we also will be establishing a relationship of trust that will thrust us into the supernatural lifestyle of God Himself—the lifestyle for which we were created.

You may or may not be facing an impossible situation in your life right now, but whatever your circumstances, God wants to invite you to follow Him on this supernatural Great Adventure. The key to answering His invitation is letting go of everything you look to for security and simply trusting Jesus instead. At first, it may feel as though you are free-falling, but you can be sure that He will catch you before you hit the ground. The more you trust Him, the more fun it gets. Before long, you will be like an excited child shouting to his or her father, "Do it again! Throw me up and catch me again!" This is the secret door to the Great Adventure—blind faith and wild trust!

# 9

# Pure Passion

Since the early 1990s, I have called Redding, California, my home base in the United States. Over the last sixteen years, I have spent little chunks of time there every few years working as a physician assistant to save money for my next overseas venture, while connecting with lifelong friends and leaders in Weaverville and Redding.

During one of these seasons, I worked at the Redding VA Outpatient Clinic. The first day I walked in, I was struck by how large the waiting room was. *Wow,* I thought, *I never realized there were so many veterans in the Redding area.* I later found out there were not that many veteran patients in Redding. The waiting room, it turned out, was a place for all the vets to hang out. I often saw men who did not have an appointment sitting in the waiting room talking with each other. Veterans from all divisions—the Marine Corps, Army, Navy, Air Force and Coast Guard—who had fought in various wars, whether WWII, the Korean War or Vietnam, all came to the clinic to socialize. They all shared a common code—the high price of pain and suffering that is foreign to most civilians. They understood each other's pain, victories and defeats, and this created a loyal intimacy so deep that they had to be together, even if it was at a doctor's office.

I often made a point to thank the vets for the price they had paid and apologize that at times my generation did not properly honor them. Some of the men cried because they had never heard anyone actually thank them for their sacrifices. On one occasion, I invited an old WWII fighter pilot to dinner with some of my friends so we could hear his stories. He was delighted to accept and showed up in uniform, with his leather flight jacket. He wept as he talked with us, moved that we actually cared to know about the price he had paid. "No one wants to listen to this," he told us. But we were listening with rapt attention. He was amazing—a real, live war hero.

These days, it seems as if the idea of sacrificing for a noble cause has fallen on hard times in Western culture. When I lived in Uzbekistan, the old men who had fought in WWII still wore their medals on their chests and received great honor in their culture. Now many American soldiers return home to indifference or even criticism. Heroism has gradually gone the way of God in our national belief system. It has been replaced by a self-centered, comfort-loving, virtueless culture. Individualism has been winning the battle for our hearts, cutting us off from the passion and nobility that only rises in us when we embrace a cause greater than ourselves. And perhaps the greatest cost is seen in the realm of relationships. Simply put, people who do not know how to sacrifice do not know how to love. They will never know the depths of human fellowship the way those veterans in that VA clinic's waiting room know it. In the words of Christ, only he who lays his life down for his friends knows such great love: "Greater love hath no man than this, that a man lay down his life for his friends" (John 15:13, KJV).

## My "Waiting Room"

I count myself especially blessed to have found a "waiting room" full of heroes who have all counted the cost and paid the price to follow the One who defined greater love. After Jesus Himself, you can have no greater treasure than friends who will take a bullet for you and who are willingly to pour out any amount of time, resources, strength and affection for you. I would not be who I am and where I am today without these friendships.

Along with the Vallottons, Harpers, Johnsons, Silks, Singhs and my other friends (some of whom I already have mentioned in these pages), two longtime residents of my "waiting room" are a dear couple I met when I first moved to the Philippines. Early on in my tenure at the YWAM clinic, I told the Lord that I wanted Him to choose my friends. He willingly obliged, though it took me a while to recognize His choice. This middle-aged couple reached out to me on many occasions, but I pushed them away because I felt intimidated by their age, sophisticated manner and affluent, professional background. Part of the reason I had been naturally drawn to minister to the poor was because I was raised in a poor, fatherless environment. I was uncomfortable with the educated and well-to-do, so when the Austins waltzed into my life, I hid from them. Hiding was a bit tricky because we lived in the same house on the mission field in the Philippines. Finally, the Lord spoke to my heart: "Remember that you wanted Me to choose your friends? Well, these are them."

I felt bad about my rudeness in avoiding the many gracious overtures the Austins made, so I went to them and apologized, admitting to my insecurity. Without missing a beat, they welcomed me into their lives and started loving, encouraging and discipling me. It still took a while for me

to really warm up to the idea that they actually liked me—
Tracy—and did not see me as some kind of project. Inside,
I thought I was too young and messed up for them to really
like me. Then one day I happened to be telling them about
my friendship with the Vallottons' children and how much
I loved them. In response, the wife asked, "Why would you
like those children? You're a generation older than they are.
You're more educated than they are."

That was when it finally clicked for me. I was not the
Austins' project, just as the Vallotton children were not my
project. The Austins actually liked me. Their love did so much
to pull me out of that poverty and orphan type of thinking
and help me see myself as a trustworthy and loved friend. It
was this couple who took me in when I returned to the States
after I left China and the Philippines, and who encouraged
and facilitated my medical education at Stanford. Later, after
my stints in Uzbekistan and Kiribati, I decided to attend
a ministry school on the East Coast while taking another
clinic job. But while driving through the deserts of Utah on
my way there, I had a high-speed accident, rolled my truck
and scattered my few possessions across the barren highway.
The police took me to the nearest town, while my truck was
towed to an auto dump. I called the Austins and explained
my situation, and they immediately wired me the money to
purchase a new truck. Time after time they bailed me out of
messes I had gotten myself into. Their friendship continues
to be one of the deepest and dearest in my life.

The same commitment and communion exists among the
men and woman with whom I now serve at my current ministry base in Mozambique, Africa. In many ways, we are a
diverse group—we come from different countries, different
languages, different denominations and different professional
backgrounds. Some are old, some are young, some are single,

some have families with kids. In any other context, I do not know that we would have chosen to live, work and spend our lives together. But we all know God chooses our families for a reason, and we all have embraced His invitation to do life together in a place where there are endless opportunities to lay our lives down for one another. The pressures we face allow us to see each other at our best and our worst, and to choose to be there for one another. Honestly, when I see the price each of my friends pays on a regular basis to serve those who cannot possibly repay them, I am humbled to be in a company of true "mighty men" like those who followed King David. Their continual loving sacrifices renew my passion to do what I must to be counted among them.

Because of the way they have inspired me, I feel strongly that this book would not be complete without introducing you to some of these heroes of mine. These radical lovers of God live with their hearts set on the prize of knowing Jesus and joining Him in His divine exploits of supernatural courage, power and extravagant love. Because they live for an audience of One, the vast majority of their exploits are not played out on a stage, recorded on video or written in a book. These saints would never draw attention to themselves. In fact, they shun the limelight, so I will change their names to protect their anonymity. But I want to introduce them to you and honor their passion, in the hope that they will inspire you as much as they have me.

## Jessie

Jessie, affectionately known as Jess among us, is a young and single, beautiful and blond Afrikaans nurse from Johannesburg, South Africa. Jess grew up during the years of apartheid, when black South Africans and white South Africans were entirely segregated. But Jess heard the invitation of Christ as a young woman and moved to black Mozambique as a medical missionary. It was not exactly the most politically correct thing for her to do, but when the Lord speaks, His disciples obey.

Jessie established a medical ministry among the Shona tribal people in central Mozambique, near a highway that runs east and west from the Indian Ocean to Zimbabwe. She lived in a rusted railway container about a kilometer's walk from this highway. Truckers often spent the night on the roadside and would transmit HIV and other tropical illnesses to some of the village women. Jessie began to care for these women, their children and the orphans left behind when the mothers died. She went from hut to hut treating patients with HIV, leprosy, tuberculosis, malaria, parasitic infections and, saddest of all, starvation.

In 2008, we built a new clinic and recovery center on that roadside. The ministry currently cares for nine hundred babies and their caregivers. The caregivers are usually aunts, sisters, teenage siblings or neighbors who volunteer to "adopt" and care for an orphaned, possibly HIV-positive child. They bring the child to the clinic once a week for a physical exam and a week's ration of milk. The caregivers are also treated if they are ill. If we can keep the caregivers alive and healthy, the orphans have a much better chance at survival.

One woman in particular who died after giving birth left behind two beautiful but malnourished twins. Jess spent countless hours nursing them in their frail state, and little by little she brought them back to health. Then one day she made the shocking decision to adopt both children as her own. To understand the full impact of Jessie's decision, you have to remember the strict social norms, political barriers and strife between the races in South Africa. Picture showing up at your white Afrikaans parents' home with two coal-black children. Imagine laying down the dream of ever getting married and having a home or children of your own. What black or white man would want to marry Jess now? The sacrifice she made to embrace these children is almost incomprehensible. In one radical act, she risked rejection by her culture and her homeland. But the most amazing part of this whole story is that she chose to adopt the twins before testing them for HIV. She did not want that factor to affect her decision. That was fourteen years ago. Today, these children are strong and beautiful, and will ever be as black as Jess is white.

Jess has continued to lay her life down for her kids, and for the nine hundred children whom we now feed every day in our nutrition program. As of the writing of this book, another eighteen hundred children have successfully graduated off the clinic/feeding program. Some would say that Jessie is too sacrificial because her giving has adversely affected her health. I became concerned for her well-being and confronted her at one point, giving her the classic airplane safety example: "You put the oxygen mask on your own face first, and then you help others." I was hoping that I could convince her to take care of herself first so she could stay healthy enough to take care of everyone else. Jessie listened intently to me, but made no promises to heed my advice.

The night after our discussion, I had a powerful encounter with God. The Lord woke me up from a dead sleep and spoke two words audibly to me: "Spend yourself." That was it. I got up and looked up the phrase in my concordance. Isaiah 58:10 says, "*Spend yourselves* in behalf of the hungry and satisfy the needs of the oppressed" (NIV, emphasis added). I noticed that it did not say, "Spend your excess cash" or "Spend what you've got stashed in the bank." It said, "Spend *yourselves*." At that point I thought, *Uh-oh. Maybe I'm the one who's missing something here.*

Jess is laying herself down for the love of these kids. There is no other reason, no one out there to impress. No one knows about her. She is spending all she is and all she has . . . all because of that incomprehensible love. Incidentally, I recently dragged Jess to a dentist myself after seeing a gaping hole in her tooth. But when the dentist examined her, both the hole and her pain had disappeared! I guess Jesus really meant it when He promised to take care of our needs when we are faithful to seek first His Kingdom. And isn't "spending yourself" exactly what Jesus did? He spent His very body and blood, willingly. In John chapter 6, Jesus miraculously fed the crowds bread and fish. Then when they came asking for more, He turned to them and said:

> I am the living bread which came down from heaven. If any-one eats of this bread, he will live forever; and the bread that I shall give is My flesh, which I shall give for the life of the world. . . . Most assuredly, I say to you, unless you eat the flesh of the Son of Man and drink His blood, you have no life in you. Whoever eats My flesh and drinks My blood has eternal life, and I will raise him up at the last day. For My flesh is food indeed, and My blood is drink indeed.
>
> John 6:51, 53–55

In essence Jesus was saying, "Go ahead, take My life. It's all yours." His love is so immense, mysterious and incom-prehensible—yet every once in a while, someone like Jessie "gets it" and follows Him, giving his or her life away.

## Bev

Bev, a behavior analyst, faithfully served with me in Mozam-bique for a season after completing her training at Bethel

School of Supernatural Ministry. You may be familiar with Gary Chapman's book *The Five Love Languages* (Northfield Publishing, 2009). Bev is fluent in them all; she is a generous gift giver, she is affectionate, she loves quality time with people and she pours out affirming words and acts of service. Bev used all the love languages extraordinarily when she was with me.

Bev and I traveled from village to village, scattering the seed of the Gospel and loving on Mozambicans in whatever way we could. On one occasion, a pastor's wife in a certain village asked us to visit a dying woman. We drove the truck as far in as we could, but the road conditions forced us to stop and walk the rest of the way to the woman's hut. As we approached, a crowd began to gather—a common occurrence when white people show up. As we neared the hut's door, an unbearable stench greeted us, literally washing over us as we stopped outside. When we entered the hut, we found the woman writhing on the dirt floor in her own excrement and bodily fluids. Withered and dying, she was clothed only in a rag.

The neighbors told us that the woman's name was Maria. Her family had already abandoned her, and her neighbors had stripped her of all her belongings, anticipating her imminent death. Maria was barely conscious, severely dehydrated and in extreme pain. We did not know what was wrong with her, but she looked as if she were in the last stages of either tuberculosis or AIDS. Bev propped Maria up and gave her a drink from her water bottle. We prayed for her, but she was not healed. We so wanted to see her jump up and praise God, as we had seen happen with others now and then in the past, but nothing happened. We decided to take her to the nearest town with a hospital.

Maria's body was like an empty sack of bones. She probably weighed less than eighty pounds. Seeing her lying in a pool of bodily fluids and blanketed with flies, nobody had wanted to touch her for fear of contracting the disease that was claiming her life. But without hesitation, Bev scooped Maria up in her arms and quickly headed for our truck. When Bev reached the vehicle, a neighbor and I held Maria gingerly while Bev climbed into the back. We put Maria on her lap to make the rugged trip softer on the dying woman.

Wide-eyed with amazement, the neighbors and pastor's wife watched everything we did. They had never seen love demonstrated like this, especially from a white woman to a black woman. They were so impacted by Bev's actions that they immediately sought out ways to demonstrate their own love to this poor woman. (Love is contagious that way.) As we headed out, a few people grabbed some food and jumped into the truck to accompany us to the hospital. Another person fetched a blanket for Maria.

Maria leaked all over Bev, but Bev did not seem to care. The road was strung together by an elaborate series of potholes, which made travel painfully slow and bumpy. Bev sat on the floorboard and leaned against the side rails, cushioning Maria from the rough ride with her own body. Maria's feces ran down Bev's lap every time we hit a pothole. Through the driver's window, I could hear Bev singing into Maria's ear as the sick woman's head rested on Bev's shoulder. Bev told her of God's great love for her, kissed her sweating cheek and stroked her matted hair.

Two of the neighbors stayed with Maria in the hospital, sleeping on the floor beneath her bed. Sadly, a few days later Maria died. They transported her body home to be buried among her own people.

The sight of Bev at that hospital will be forever etched in my memory. For me, she was a vision of Christ in us, the hope of glory! With Maria's diarrhea and urine streaking down her skirt, Bev smiled from ear to ear as she observed Maria through a window, resting in a clean bed in the hospital room. Plenty of people would have called her crazy for showing such disregard for herself in risking her own health. But Bev did not care if she caught a contagious disease, and she was not moved by what people thought of her. She just loved people like Maria supernaturally, as Jesus did. Jesus often healed the sick by simply speaking the word, yet almost every time He healed lepers, He touched them. Jesus knew how to heal their rejected hearts as well as their diseased bodies.

**Helen**

Helen is another of our nurses in the clinic. Like Jess, she is saving lives every day. Most of the children she serves will never know that this highly educated woman left her family, abandoned her career in Europe and gave up marriage opportunities just to serve them. She worked in intensive care for one and a half years in the beautiful town of Darmstadt just so she could save enough money to support herself in Mozambique. She was a young Christian with no church supporting her, but she was intensely single-minded and committed to the Lord's call on her life. To prepare to serve in Mozambique, she moved to Portugal to first learn the language. From there, she moved to Liverpool to take one of the top tropical medicine courses in the world. When she arrived in Mozambique, she had only been a Christian for three years. After nine years of riots, snakes, malaria and countless hardships and adventures, she is still serving the African people with intense passion.

One day, I was sitting at tea with Helen when a riot broke out just outside our house. (Many riots take place where we live, but this happened to be the same instance Kris mentioned in his introduction, when I called him for prayer in the midst of gunfire.) The town was taking a stand against corruption in the police force, and it was not long before bullets began to fly. The din became so loud that Helen and I had to shout at each other to be heard, yet neither of us ever broke down and took off in fear for our lives. We held our ground, silently reaffirming to one another that we were not afraid of death and would stick together as we committed ourselves to God. It was a beautiful moment for both of us because it revealed what was in our hearts.

Now and then the nurses find children abandoned at the clinic who are in the last stages of a deadly disease. They take them home, often staying up through the night to care for them. Some children at death's door have been healed— sometimes supernaturally, sometimes through medical and nutritional intervention—but all through the missionaries' loving hands and compassionate hearts. Others are not as fortunate and die in pain, often crying deep into the night, while these nurses do their best to comfort them until they finally slip into the hands of God.

## Judy

Judy is a Bethel School graduate and a primary school teacher. When she joined our team, we really did not have a ministry that fit her gift mix. She could not serve in the clinic because she had no medical training. And I certainly could not put such a young, pretty woman in our prison ministry! But she is a very mature, proactive believer, so we told her to create her own niche, promising that we would provide safe housing, a visa and some basic infrastructure. She decided to raise support and build a school. It has turned into an incredible success. She teaches children from predominantly Muslim families and has gained so much favor within the Muslim community that they have welcomed her into their homes wholeheartedly. She has led her students to Christ and started a children's church with around two hundred kids.

Judy is young and wants to get married. Before she came to Mozambique, we talked extensively about her dreams and goals. I told her quite frankly to stay at Bethel if marriage was really her primary passion, because she was not likely to find the man of her dreams in the outbacks of Mozambique. She came anyway. "I'll trust God for my husband," she said confidently. Sure enough, she met the man of her dreams when he came to Mozambique on an outreach. Now they are engaged!

These are just a few of several missionaries who continually go the extra mile in the harsh African conditions to serve the people of Mozambique day in and day out. I have mentioned the fact that Bev, Jess, Helen and Judy made choices that, as far as they could see, severely limited their marriage prospects. This demonstrates that true passion requires us to choose one goal above all others. Passion may have many manifestations, but it must maintain a narrow focus to capture its divine purpose. When conflict arises between our desires, we must prioritize our passions or we will find ourselves paralyzed by indecision. Thankfully, as Judy's story shows, God's promise is true—when we choose to delight in Him above all, He will faithfully fulfill the desires of our hearts, either here, in heaven or both.

We also work with single guys, married couples and young and not-so-young missionaries who come to Mozambique from far and wide. We are a very eclectic group of international and interdenominational Jesus lovers, every one of whom has willingly paid a huge price to serve in this tough environment. Everyone has suffered recurring bouts of malaria and other tropical illnesses and injuries. Most have been robbed or victimized in different ways. All of our team members have endured false accusations, suspicion and rejection. But, like the apostle Paul, we press on to take hold of that for which Christ Jesus took hold of us (see Philippians 3:12).

## The Fellowship of Suffering

I fervently hope that you are as rich in true friends and family as I am blessed to be. If not, I highly recommend that you ask God to bring them into your life. But when you do, remember this: Many of our moments of deepest intimacy with the Lord occur at the "table" He prepares for us in the valley of the shadow of death. Likewise, so will our deepest covenant friendships be tested and forged in moments of suffering and loss. I know this is not a popular topic, and we should not seek to glorify suffering. But we would be foolish not to prepare our hearts to face it when it comes so that we can gain the growth and beauty of what suffering brings.

Over the past thirty years, I have lost nine close missionary friends. All of my friends in Mozambique also have lost loved ones. In my earlier years in Asia, I buried hundreds of children whom we could not save from the ravages of disease and malnutrition. Those of us working with each other in such conditions have had many opportunities to grieve together, to move closer in the midst of pain. It is difficult to describe the heart connection these times have forged among us.

Of course, the only thing that has enabled us to endure suffering together is that we depend on the One who has already "borne our griefs and carried our sorrows" (Isaiah 53:4). He gives us the strength to carry on, the words of life to speak to each other and the hope and healing our hearts desperately need. But we also understand that these moments are priceless opportunities where He allows us to share in "the fellowship of His sufferings" (Philippians 3:10). We get another inkling of what He experienced on the cross for us, and it reveals the depth of His love in a way that nothing else can.

I hear some people say, "We're on the other side of the cross now. Let's stop talking about His suffering and death so much." But as one person pointed out, the scars on Christ's body are the only man-made things in heaven. His resurrected, glorified body in which He can walk through walls and ascend to heaven still bears the marks of His sacrifice—scars that eternally proclaim His extravagant, demonstrative love for us. I like to think that the same will be true of those who share in the "fellowship of His sufferings" in this life. One of my favorite poems, written by Amy Carmichael, asks:

> Hast thou no scar?
> No hidden scar on foot, or side or hand?
> I hear thee sung as mighty in the land,
> I hear them hail thy bright ascendant star,
> Hast thou no scar?
>
> Hast thou no wound?
> Yet I was wounded by the archers, spent,
> Leaned me against a tree to die; and rent
> By ravening beasts that encompassed Me, I swooned.
> Hast thou no wound?
>
> No wound? No scar?
> Yet, as the Master shall the servant be,
> And pierced are the feet that follow Me;
> But thine are whole: can he have followed far
> Who has no wound nor scar?[1]

1. "Hast Thou No Scar?" in *Toward Jerusalem* by Amy Carmichael, Copyright 1955 by The Dohnavur Fellowship, and administered by CLC Ministries International, publisher. Used by permission of CLC Publications. All rights reserved.

If you faithfully stick with Him—and with the brothers and sisters He has called you to walk with to the end—you will have scars. But you will also have glory. As Paul said, "The Spirit Himself bears witness with our spirit that we are children of God, and if children, then heirs—heirs of God and joint heirs with Christ, if indeed we suffer with Him, that we may also be glorified together" (Romans 8:16–17). The level of pain we experience when others suffer is the true measurement of the depth of love we have for one another. The fear of suffering has relegated many people to a life of independence and isolation. But love suffers long, and Jesus draws near to the brokenhearted. If you want to experience true intimacy and you hunger to be loved, you will only find it in the family affair of the cross.

# 10

# Bringing Orphans Home

I probably will never get over the irony of God giving me, a single woman who eschewed marriage and children because she frankly never felt suited for them, over nine hundred children whom I help provide for and feed. He has called me, a girl who grew up hardly knowing her father, to carry the message of adoption and fatherhood to a fatherless nation. I guess that is just how He works; He picks the most unlikely candidate and does His wonders. He set the lonely—me—in a family, and now He has asked me to extend that family to other lonely ones. And it is our greatest privilege and joy to freely give away what we have so freely received.

In addition to feeding and caring for orphans, we also have a thriving prison ministry in two towns in Mozambique. Every two or three months, a new group of men (and a few women) are sentenced to these prisons. Most of them have no idea who their fathers are, so when I introduce myself to them for the first time, I start by telling them a story. I say, "Guys, there's good news. Did you know the president is in town today?"

"You're kidding!" they respond. "Why is he here?"

"Well," I say, "it so happened that when the president was a young man, he fell in love with the girl of his dreams. They married, and they had a son. But a rival kidnapped the son and fled with him. All these years this man has been looking for his son, especially since he became the president. When the boy was very little, he fell and hit his head on the fireplace, so he has a very odd scar on his brow. A guard in this prison once served the president years ago. He now works here as a guard, and he has recognized that one of you has this unique scar. So the president is here to look at the scar and see if its owner is his true son. Isn't that cool?"

It is not long before they realize that I am just telling them a tale. So I admit, "Yes, I'm just telling you a fun story. But wouldn't it be great if the president walked in here, pointed to you and said, 'You are my son. I see it in your eyes. You belong to me. I'm taking you out of this prison and I'm paying your fine for you. I'm taking you to the royal palace in Maputo.'"

They all agree, "Yes, that would be wonderful!"

So I say, "The president may not be your father, but you do have a Father, and He is greater than any king or president." Then I introduce them to their Father in heaven, who created them and sent Jesus to take them back from the clutches of their unlawful abductors, sin and the devil. I tell them, "Today is the day He will save you from the prison of shame and guilt in your heart. You are loved. You are not forsaken or forgotten. But as a son, you have a choice to make. Will you walk out of this prison with Him, or would you rather remain behind the rusted bars of captivity?"

Every time I give this invitation, the men begin weeping like children, and they all get saved. I do not know how long it has been since we had a prisoner who was not saved. Every day we come back and reinforce the message and reality of their adoption. These men are underfed—most of them are just skin and bones, and some are too weak to stand. They are crawling with scabies, lice and parasites, and most are dying of diseases like AIDS and tuberculosis. They have a hole in the floor for a toilet and have not had a shower in months. We go through the room, shake their hands and hug them, making sure to touch everyone. They have really never heard good news in their lives, so their hunger is bottomless—they drink it up like dying men in the desert. We could stay there morning, noon and night and it would not be enough for these men. In their desperation for relationship and love, they do not argue or challenge. They just say, "Tell me more."

I have also used the message of adoption to reach members of the Zionist church—a syncretistic cult with elements of Christianity as well as witchcraft, ancestral worship and animism. A lot of what they believe and practice is demonic. I once visited a Zionist congregation and, knowing they have an extreme reverence for their ancestors, I asked them, "Who are your ancestors?"

They began going around and calling out the names of their parents. A few also named their grandparents, but then they had to stop. That was as far back as they knew, because the recent civil war had destroyed their heritage. They did not even know whom they were worshiping. So then I asked them, "Well, who was the very first father?"

"God," they replied.

That was my open door. "God is a jealous God," I said, "and He is jealous that you are worshiping lesser ancestors, when He is the first and truest Father of all. There's a holy jealousy and an unholy jealousy." I pointed at the priest and his wife. "If a man makes a pass at your wife, for example, you have a right to be jealous, because that jealousy protects your relationship. That woman has made a covenant with you. But if that man makes a pass at me, you have no right to be jealous, because I don't belong to you. There is no covenant between us."

I could see that they understood. I had drawn them in, so I continued, "We have a covenant with God. We're made in His image, we're His children and He has a right to be jealous of that relationship. But you are worshiping lesser fathers, mere dead men."

After hearing this simple message, the entire congregation got on their knees and repented. The whole church turned to Christ in one meeting's time. They were so hungry to know who their Father was that it was a simple matter of introducing Him and His Son to them. Later, they painted Jesus (as they see Him) on the back wall of their church. They are now reading the Bible voraciously and growing continuously in their new relationship with the only Ancestor worthy of their worship.

From the outside, the fathering and mothering we are doing in Mozambique appears one-sided, just as the relationship between parents and babies often appears one-sided. But as any loving parent experiences, the child is not the only person receiving something in the relationship. As missionaries, we feel like the privileged ones. We receive incredible joy and fulfillment by stepping into our destinies as spiritual parents, and we are constantly blessed ourselves by the things our prisoners, our babies, our schoolchildren and our tribal churches draw out of us. Their hunger stirs up revelation in the Word and brings us ideas we have never had before.

Above all, we feel privileged because we love Jesus and find Him in them. We find Him in the prisoners and the beggars. We find Him in the babies who at first are stiff because they have not been loved, but who start laughing, talking and making eye contact as the missionary nurses hold, feed, clothe and love them. When we touch these babies, we touch Him. When we feed them, we feed Him. When we clothe them, we clothe Him. And when we see their joy, it feels as though Jesus Himself is smiling and laughing back at us. Jesus said that when we have done it to the least of these, we have done it to Him. There is no greater privilege and pleasure than to share in our Father's incredible delight in His children.

### Training in Generosity

As fathers and mothers, our vision is not to make our Mozambican family dependent on us, but to help them mature into fathers and mothers who can break the curses of fatherlessness and poverty off their own people. For this reason, one of the primary foundation stones we are working to lay in their lives is generosity. We are teaching people who have almost nothing how to give. It sounds almost wrong, but the only way to break the poverty spirit is to give your way out of it. When we distribute food to the prisoners, for example, we have them practice generosity by handing their portion to someone else and receiving a portion from one of their brothers. We also teach them about tithing and invite them to tithe of their bread.

Some time ago, one of our property managers, a Muslim who came to Christ, built a home on land owned by Muslims. It took two years of his salary and work on his off-hours to finish it, and just when he had, the Muslims seized the house and kicked him and his family off the property. The timing could not have been worse. It was right before the rainy season, which is also the start of the hunger season. On payday the man came in for his wages, and I immediately saw his distress. He told me that his family was now homeless and destitute. "How are we going to survive?" he asked.

I gathered the rest of the local staff, who had all come in for payday, for a meeting. I said, "I want to talk to you about how you can build wealth. You can work for a wage and save. You can also inherit wealth if your fathers leave behind an inheritance. And you can position yourself so that God blesses you." I quoted various Scriptures about sowing and reaping, generosity and promises about inheriting God's blessing. Then I pulled out my car keys and asked, "Would you like this truck if I give it to you as a gift?"

Everyone nodded.

"But most of you can't drive," I pointed out. "If I give one of you this truck, you will probably kill yourself and some of us too. I can give it to Carlos, though, because he knows how to drive. He's mature and responsible, and he's not a drunkard. I can trust him with these keys, and you see him driving every day."

"Our Father wants to bless us," I continued, "Just like you want to bless your own children. But He's waiting for us to grow up so that the amazing things He has for us don't kill us. One of the biggest ways we can grow up is by being generous. When He knows He can trust us to steward His resources to bless others, then the windows of heaven will open. Today we have an opportunity to practice generosity. Our brother has just lost his home. You all know what that means in hunger season. He has a large family to shelter and feed. Let's take up an offering to help him. Not only will we help him; we will send a message to our town. This entire Muslim community will see how the Muslims deal with you and how the Christians deal with you."

I placed a bucket in a discreet place where their contributions would not be visible to anyone else. I said, "This is between you and God. You don't have to impress me or each other. Just know that I will match whatever you put in there." Two of the other missionaries chimed in and said they would also match the total offering. The staff all gave extravagantly.

We raised enough money for the man to build a new home on some property near our clinic, and then we gave him a month off to finish it.

Soon after, I went to visit this man's property and saw that in addition to the new house, a bunch of bricks were going up for another structure. "What's that?" I asked him.

"I'm building a church," he said. "There are more and more Christians in this village now, and we need a place of our own to worship. We need to prepare a place for God's glory to rest in our village."

I was impressed. He never asked for more money to make this happen. I knew him to be uneducated, illiterate and only barely acquainted with the basic teachings of his new faith. But he understood about preparing a place of worship and about returning the generosity of others.

I greatly anticipate seeing the blessing God will certainly entrust to these sons and daughters who are rising up with His heart to father and bless their communities and nation. This blessing and calling is not just for the poor; it is for all of us who have chosen Him. Regardless of what your life entails right now, your job is to use whatever gift God has given you to bring spiritual orphans home by reconciling the world back to Christ, just as Christ reconciled you and me back to Himself:

> Now all things are of God, who has reconciled us to Himself through Jesus Christ, and has given us the ministry of reconciliation, that is, that God was in Christ reconciling the world to Himself, not imputing their trespasses to them, and has committed to us the word of reconciliation.
>
> Now then, we are ambassadors for Christ, as though God were pleading through us: we implore you on Christ's behalf, be reconciled to God.
>
> 2 Corinthians 5:18–20

# 11

# The Real World

I love the supernatural—God's supernatural. I honestly do not know how believers can stay believers without experiencing the ongoing invasions of God's eternal reality into our temporal reality. The moment we begin to marginalize the miraculous in the here and now is the moment we begin to limit the nothing-is-impossible Almighty God we claim to worship.

I am well aware that the miraculous is often surrounded by controversy and counterfeits. I have seen charlatans fake a miracle in order to deceive and manipulate onlookers. On several occasions in Africa, I have heard people give testimony to being healed of a disease, then at the same meeting, they have come up and asked me for medicine for that disease. However, I have also seen a great number of authentic, verifiable miracles, which have been both celebrated by believers and mocked by unbelievers. Yet despite all the dust and drama, I am not going to stop bearing witness to what I have seen with my own eyes.

### Resurrection Bus

In 2004, I witnessed a resurrection. Before I tell you the story, I will mention that in my thirty-some years of running clinics in developing countries, I have had a great deal of experience with the dying and the dead, and with people's misunderstandings about them. The people with whom I live and work in Africa are uneducated. If someone passes out due to heat or illness, sometimes others will think the person has died. After lying flat for a moment and allowing circulation to return to his or her head, the person will wake up again, and onlookers will sometimes think that the person died and rose to life again. Similarly, a patient waking from a coma or a head trauma will sometimes mistakenly be reported to have been resurrected. But in the story I am about to tell you, neither I nor the other eyewitnesses had any confusion about what we had seen. A dead woman came to life again before our eyes. Frankly, it was one of the scariest things I have ever seen.

The morning of that unforgettable day, I suited up in an ambulance uniform and got into a new ambulance that I was driving back from South Africa to our clinic in Mozambique. The vehicle was not yet outfitted with medical equipment; it was basically an empty shell. But I figured wearing the uniform would help facilitate a quicker passage through the border and customs. Little did I know that the ambulance would see its first emergency that very afternoon.

About an hour before I reached the Mozambican border, a minibus ahead of me suddenly had a tire blowout. The wheel tore apart from the rim, and I watched with sickening horror as the bus, which had been traveling at 100 kilometers per hour, swerved off the road and flipped over again and again. As you can imagine, with each violent revolution the bus began to peel apart as the glass and sheet metal slammed into the earth. The bus continued to spin, and I caught glimpses of people being tossed around inside like rag dolls. What felt like an hour of horror actually took only a few seconds.

Suddenly, the bodies of two women, both of whom were clutching something to their chests, catapulted through the windshield. The women came crashing down on the rocky roadside, heads first. Then even more passengers flew from the other windows.

I immediately pulled the ambulance over, jumped out and ran toward the bus. Within moments, I was joined by quite a few other travelers who stopped to help. Being in uniform, everyone assumed I was in charge, so I took the lead in this disaster response. There was no time to hesitate. "You and you," I pointed, "go down the road and stop the oncoming traffic. The rest of you, help me with the victims. My ambulance is new and I don't have supplies, so we need to call in several ambulances."

The people scattered at my commands, rushing to do their part. Right away, we went to work assessing the damage. The scene was gruesome. We counted eighteen victims, a few of whom were still trapped inside the overturned bus—and some were even pinned underneath it.

My first priority was the two women I had seen go airborne through the windshield. I was shocked to see that the bundles in their arms were babies, and even more shocked that the infants were both still alive and unharmed. Sadly, the same could not be said of the two mothers; they had cushioned the babies' falls with their own bodies. After landing on their heads, the women were flipped onto their backs and sprawled out on the rocks. Somehow one was still alive, but just barely. The other had not survived. Her neck was clearly broken, and her head had twisted almost completely around so that her face was lying on the ground in a large pool of blood. Her temporal skull was indented, and her right eye had popped out of its socket and was resting on her cheek, hanging by its optic nerve. She had no pulse and no respiration. She was dead. I covered her head with a shirt that was lying nearby.

One of the loveliest, most courageous acts of love I have ever seen unfolded before me as I tended to the two mangled mothers. One of the victims, a Zulu woman with many injuries, including a bleeding, compound fracture of her right femur, saw the two babies and crawled on her elbows through the rocks to reach them. When she reached the two women, she pried the babies out of their mothers' arms. Then she rolled onto her back on the rocks, threw up her blouse and began to breastfeed and comfort the babies. Stunned by this act of kindness in the midst of obvious suffering, I asked, "Oh! Do you know these women?"

"No," she said. "I am just trying to help."

I was blown away. Most women, particularly Zulu women, would never nurse a stranger's baby on the roadside. A strong cultural taboo exists against doing such a thing, as they believe it could expose the woman to any curses that rest on that baby, or vice versa. This woman, however—in extreme pain and in a life-and-death crisis—broke with her own cultural norms, abandoned concern for her own physical and spiritual well-being and comforted two strangers' babies. I will never forget that moment.

Shortly thereafter, a white Afrikaans woman ran up to help me with the two mothers. "I just don't want to touch them," she said.

I understood. Because of widespread HIV and AIDS in Africa, most people are very cautious about exposing themselves to another person's blood. Unfortunately, it is difficult to help an injured person without touching him or her. I decided I would just ask this Afrikaans woman and the other "no touch" helpers to pray. A good many South Africans, both white and black, grew up in church, so I was pretty sure they would have no problem with that.

"Everyone, listen!" I yelled. "Start praying for these people. I want you to pray out loud over and over again, 'God, heal and preserve life here today, in Jesus' name.' Every time I look at you, I want to see your lips moving!"

After issuing this order, I went back to my rounds, running from patient to patient. I assessed their needs, compressed their bleeds and calmed their panic while waiting for the real ambulances and EMTs to arrive. A group of men finally managed to rock the bus over while others pulled more victims from underneath it. Everywhere people were calling to me, asking me what to do next and taking my instructions. The scene was mayhem. And then it happened . . .

While tending to a victim twenty or thirty feet from the dead woman, I heard that first Afrikaans lady yell to me, "Sister, come back over here and help this lady!"

"She's already dead," I yelled back. "I have all these others to look after."

But she insisted, "Come! She's breathing again!"

That got my attention. I looked back at her in disbelief. What I saw was nothing less than terrifying. With the shirt still covering her head, the dead woman first sat up, and then rotated her head around to face forward again.

We all began to scream. A few of the helpers took off running, and I heard their cars peeling out a few seconds later. I was scared witless, but somehow from some deep recess I mustered the courage to run over to the woman. I removed the bloodied shirt from her head and jumped back. Though her face was still covered with blood, her eye was miraculously back in its socket, and her head was no long misshapen. She coughed up some blood, spat it out, and then began to look around and call out for her baby. She was alive!

"She is alive again!" I yelled to the others. "Pray for your patients!"

A roar of prayer went up everywhere. I ran to another woman who looked to be about eight months pregnant. Lying on the ground, she was hardly breathing and visibly in pain. She had fractured some ribs. I asked her, "Do you believe Jesus can heal you and your baby?"

Unable to catch her breath to speak, she just nodded. We prayed together. Within moments, she began to take full breaths and move her body without pain. She rose to her feet, grinning at me with tearful joy. She was completely healed! With a deep mighty voice that only Africans have, she burst out in praise and then rushed over to pray for others. I learned later that she was a radical believer in Jesus.

Fourteen of the eighteen casualties were completely healed that day as we waited two and a half hours for the other ambulances to reach us from town. Not one life was lost. Five unconscious patients with severe head injuries were all healed. Many of the healed patients had cell phones and called their loved ones for a lift. Since they were from farms in that area, many went home rather than riding back to the county hospital. I am sure the EMTs were a bit confused by the scene when they arrived, as it looked nothing like what they had been told. The Lord had already done the work!

As I drove away in my empty ambulance, I marveled at what I had witnessed—I marvel to this day. I have prayed for many dead to rise to life, and to date it has not happened. The one time I did not pray, a dead woman came back to life. And I must confess, when I asked those stopping by to pray that God would preserve lives and heal, I was merely hoping that no others would die from their injuries while waiting for the ambulances. We were a long way from town, and several had serious head and body trauma that could have resulted in imminent death. I was in medical mode, not supernatural mode. Yet the Lord had mercy on us all and surpassed our wildest expectations, as He so brilliantly does. What a mighty God we serve!

## Milk without Money

As we see in the ministry of Jesus, sometimes God puts His power on display for all to see, and sometimes He keeps it almost entirely hidden. Jesus boldly healed men on the Sabbath in front of all the Pharisees, purposely devastating all their religious boxes and stirring up controversy. Other times, Jesus quietly touched a person and instructed him not to broadcast the news of the healing. As much as I love the obvious displays of God's power, like that woman's resurrection, I am also constantly aware that He is working behind the scenes, doing far more than I can imagine. In fact, like the Israelites living on supernatural bread from heaven for forty years, I believe everything my friends and I are doing in Africa is completely dependent upon the supernatural power and provision of God. We are living in a miracle, and I never want to forget it.

Jess, Helen and I started our current clinic for orphans in a big Army tent out on the roadside. The day we were putting up the tent, a British man visiting friends down the road walked by and asked what we were doing. When we explained that we were opening a clinic for children, he said we could not do a clinic out of a tent and then gave us £8,000 to build our clinic. We were extremely grateful for the money, but a building was not what we needed most.

Our biggest need—and the thing that was actually saving lives—was milk. So we asked this man, "Can we use this money for milk?"

He said, "No, it is for a building," so we built a clinic.

Milk has always been our most difficult expense to meet. We all agreed to trust God for the supplies to meet the needs of the now nine hundred babies and their caregivers whom we look after. He has stretched that trust beyond what we ever imagined when we started, and He continues to supernaturally supply our needs.

Around this time, God spoke to me through Isaiah 55:1 about "buying milk without money." That verse says, "Come, all you who are thirsty, come to the waters; and you who have no money, come, buy and eat! Come, buy wine and milk without money and without cost" (NIV). With each new baby on the program, the Lord grows our faith and meets our needs. But this verse in Isaiah birthed a sense that He had something even more spectacular planned to fulfill this promise of "milk without money."

Sure enough, in the summer of 2011 He kept that promise. As we approached having nine hundred infants in our program, we found ourselves facing a fairly serious crisis with our milk supply. In faith, I made the two-day drive through Zimbabwe into South Africa to buy milk—again, as I had done on many occasions—without the money to pay for it. Before, it had somehow always worked out, despite the lack of fund-raising or a website or newsletters asking for support. But this time there was no milk—the entire Sub-Sahara of Africa was in the midst of a milk shortage. My heart was in my throat for an entire week. I could hardly speak for fear of having a major meltdown, and my sleep was more than tormenting. I kept having nightmares of burying hundreds of babies, as had happened before when I worked in Asia, all because of a simple lack of milk. *God, where are You now?* I asked.

We had only a few bags of milk left when I received news that a milk company in South Africa had received a shipment. By that point, I had enough cash to buy a five-day supply. Four solid days of driving, all the way to South Africa and back, for five days of milk is very much like trying to feed the five thousand with two fishes and five loaves, but we had to make the trip.

My friend Jess hardly spoke on that two-day drive south. Upon arriving in South Africa, we spent the night with Jess's friends. In the morning, these friends announced that they would like to help us purchase the load of milk and asked us how much it would cost. I was embarrassed to tell them that a week's supply cost $2,300. "Any amount toward that would be such a help," I said, thinking they would perhaps give $100.

The wife said, "I was thinking of giving $10,700. Stop by my husband's office on the way to the milk company and pick up the check."

Jess and I literally danced out to the truck. By the time we got to her husband's office, however, the amount had grown to $14,100, enough to buy several weeks' worth of milk! With the cash we had brought with us, we were able to add twenty tins of formula for the kids who were lactose intolerant. Even more beautiful was the precise way in which the Lord fulfilled His word to me about buying milk without money. We did just that—this South African couple wired the money directly into the milk company's account. I simply ordered the milk and picked it up without paying a cent.

Through the simple assignment of giving milk to babies, God has been teaching my friends and me to build our lives in the realm of faith where we cannot simply hope for miracles, we must count on them. It is a life-or-death kind of faith. The stakes are very high, but He is faith-*full*. The moment God withdraws His supernatural supply from us, we will dry up. Thus far, we have always had just enough to meet the growing needs of our growing numbers, and we will continue to move forward as long as He says to do so. We are well aware that by Western standards, what we are doing is not "sustainable." People from the States will ask what our budget looks like, and I have to tell them frankly, "We spend whatever we have as soon as we have it." We cannot say of some reserve cash, "Oh, that money is untouchable—it's for tomorrow." If we do not use next month's resources for this month, there may not be people to minister to next month.

The people we serve live each day as if it were their last, because often it is. Though the Mozambican economy is rapidly improving, it is still the sixth-poorest nation in the world, and each month we face the possibility of famine, starvation, natural disasters, epidemics or civil unrest. Some have asked us, "What if it all dries up?"

"Well," we answer, "then it dries up and we have had the privilege of feeding these hundreds of people for all these years."

It is not as if what we have accomplished will have no value. After all, one day I am going to die, and dying someday will not cancel the value of my life today. What will cancel the value of my life is refusing to trust God.

### Fear Is a Pretender

Nothing shuts down our hearts and keeps us from stepping into a supernatural lifestyle more than fear. If we were created to do divine exploits, then fear is obviously the opposite of what we were made for, because it destroys our hopes, infects our thoughts, robs our potential and kills us off little by little. Fear is dehumanizing.

Some years ago I had an experience that will forever remind me of the nature of fear. Before I joined Jess, Helen and the rest of my current ministry partners, I worked with Iris Ministries in Maputo, Mozambique. My visa expired every month, so I had to make regular trips to South Africa to renew it. The highway between Maputo and Johannesburg runs right along the border of Kruger Park, one of the largest and most beautiful animal parks in the world. My desire to visit the park grew with each monthly journey, but for six years I never had the time or money to go. Finally, a friend kidnapped me on my birthday and surprised me with a one-day safari through Kruger.

Once I realized where we were heading, I started to put in my order with God for the animals I wanted to see: "I want to see the zebra, the elephant, the cheetah, the water buffalo, the leopard . . ." Kruger Park is the size of Switzerland, and it is possible to be there all day without seeing much of anything. I wanted to give God plenty of time to round up all the animals for me. Wonderfully, the day turned out perfectly—I saw everything on my list . . . everything except the leopard.

That night, my friend and I stayed at a hotel just outside the park. I woke up early the next morning and discovered that our hotel had bicycles to rent. It was winter and pretty chilly out, but a bike ride sounded like the perfect way to warm up. I pedaled out onto the main road running parallel to a park fence. As I rode and gazed out over the landscape, I thanked God for all I had seen the day before, marveling at His wild creativity and handiwork. "But I really did want to see a leopard," I told Him with just the tiniest bit of disappointment. "I specifically requested a leopard, and it wasn't in the lineup."

As I was discussing this with the Lord, I heard rustling and growling coming from some brush along the fence up ahead. I slowed down to look. As I passed the spot, to my astonishment I saw a leopard with its head caught under the fence wire. The crouching animal jumped back a bit, apparently startled by me. Then it lunged right under the fence and took off after me like a shot!

In terror, I pumped my bike pedals for dear life. Thankfully I was on a steep downhill and was already riding quickly, but in my heart I knew it was no use—leopards are the fastest land creatures on earth. A split-second backward glance confirmed that it was gaining on me, though strangely, instead of the usual sleek shape of a big cat, this leopard was somewhat fat.

*Great!* I thought. *It's a monster leopard!* I pressed forward with everything in me, my heart pounding in my throat and my legs aching. Looking forward, I could see another hazard lying at the bottom of the hill just a few hundred yards ahead of us—a busy intersection in the highway. My mind quickly raced for an answer. Should I risk riding through the traffic in hopes that the leopard would get smashed and not me? Or should I stop and face my pursuer? At the last minute I decided. As I reached the bottom of the hill just before the intersection, I slammed on my brakes, jumped off the bike, whipped out my pepper spray and prepared for the worst. My heart was pumping so hard that I thought I was going to pass out.

To my surprise, I had put a bit of distance between myself and the pursuing beast. In fact, I registered with disbelief that the creature was slowing down, and most shocking of all, it was not a leopard! The fearsome monster I had been ready to rip through a busy intersection to escape was nothing more than a big Boxer dog wearing a winter leopard-print dog sweater. By the time it trotted up to me, it was as tired as I was and was wheezing, with its tongue hanging from the side of its mouth. Obviously exhausted, it stopped and lay down on the roadside, waiting for me to pet it. I collapsed to the ground myself in exhaustion, relief and embarrassment. I felt so foolish. *Be careful what you wish for*, I thought. *You just might get it.*

It struck me that what had just happened to me was exactly what so often happens to us all. Our enemies and problems come chasing after us like roaring lions, but they are just pretenders. They try to get us to react—to fight, flee or freeze—and each of these classic reactions can impair our thinking and perception. Sometimes these pretenders only make us look foolish, but sometimes they get us to do really stupid things—things that will totally sabotage our lives and our destinies.

I would rather die boldly than live as a coward. I would rather take a step, even in presumption, than stay frozen in uncertainty and insecurity. Too many times I have stalled out in mediocrity, thinking I was waiting for God, when actually I was just hiding in fear. As someone once said, you cannot steer a car unless it is moving. I have come to trust that God will guide me, but unless I am in motion, He will not do what He does best! And I learned that God has a marvelous sense of humor—a leopard-dog . . . really?

## One Step at a Time

For you, reading the stories in these pages and thinking about what you would do in the midst of hardship or chaos may have left you feeling hopeless. If you feel it is hopeless that you will ever be able to rise up to some idealistic spiritual status, let me be clear—being fearless and passionate does not mean that you remain in a state of exuberance, or that you are always in some noble battle. As William Carey, the father of missions, pointed out, running the race is actually more a matter of faithful plodding than sprinting.

Most of the time when Jess, Helen and the others are feeding our nine-hundredth baby, or I am driving a truck to South Africa to buy milk, we are not intensely aware that we are doing something supernatural or divinely inspired. But when we take a step back, we can see how His love fills our hearts and inspires us to pour out our lives for others. I personally love the fact that Jesus was more impressed with the widow's mite than He was with any big offering. Our Father is searching for champions who will give their two cents for God's sake and push past their fear.

## God of Wonders

Believe me, if you say "yes" to walking with the God of Wonders, you will see Him put His power on display in and around you. What is more, He will require you to take step after step with nothing more to stand on than His promise that He will show up and do the impossible. It will be frightening, messy, controversial and mind-blowing. But it will definitely be anything but boring. It will be real—reality itself crashing in. God wants to teach His sons and daughters to live in that reality—to live as He does. He wants His normal to become our normal.

The more we learn to live as Jesus did, only doing and saying what the Father does and says, the more we will be living from passion, from our hearts. We will not be like small children, dependent on their parents to direct their every move. Rather, because we have committed ourselves to love what our Father loves, we understand that He trusts us to make decisions and is more than happy to back us up. This would not be the case if we had a competing agenda, of course. But our hearts beat in time with His, so why would He not want to fulfill what is in our hearts? Jesus put it like this, "If you abide in Me, and My words abide in you, ask whatever you wish, and it will be done for you" (John 15:7, NASB).

The story of Jonathan and his armor-bearer illustrates this beautifully. The Philistines had so oppressed Israel that the only ones left with any weapons were King Saul and his son Jonathan. But instead of Jonathan camping out with his dad and waiting for something to happen, he took it on himself to face the Philistines in battle. He did not have a word from God; he was just fed up with seeing his country oppressed, so he decided to do something about it. He said to his armor-bearer: "Come, let us go over to the garrison of these uncircumcised; it may be that the LORD will work for us. For nothing restrains the LORD from saving by many or by few" (1 Samuel 14:6).

I love his armor-bearer's response: "Do all that is in your heart. Go then; here I am with you, according to your heart" (verse 7). I also like the fact that Jonathan said, "Maybe God will help us," because I feel that way so often. I find myself having to decide important issues in life and ministry without having a definitive word from God. In these situations, I have to trust what He has already sown in my heart. Jonathan's heart was to trust God and face his enemy boldly. When he did what was in his heart, he stepped into the supernatural. The Lord defended him, and the entire Philistine army was defeated!

We were created to be like Jonathan—to live from our hearts, free from fear. When our passion for the Lord is our guide, we step into the superior reality of life with God. We were not called just to be survivors. We were divinely designed to do exploits. Paul wrote, "For we are God's handiwork, created in Christ Jesus to do good works, which God prepared in advance for us to do" (Ephesians 2:10, NIV).

That phrase "good works" is the same one Jesus used to describe His own divine exploits—healing the sick, cleansing lepers, casting out demons, raising the dead and preaching the Good News to the poor. These are the "works" that evidence our partnership with the living God (see John 14:12). When we begin to live from our hearts and pursue our true passion, these supernatural signs will follow us.

# Epilogue

## Kris Vallotton

It seems to me that when many of us hear a story like Tracy's, it prompts one of two responses—either we are so awed by her exploits that we place her on a pedestal that cannot be humanly obtained, or we digress into guilt and shame, overcome by our own lack of courageous exploits. Thus we fade away into a world of powerless living.

Yet our goal for recording Tracy's life of adventure is not to impress you, nor is it to shame you. *Not at all!* Rather, her life is meant to inspire you. Our prayer is that you would come to realize that if someone as ordinary as Tracy can live such an extraordinary life, then so can you.

I am convinced that we were *all* created for adventure. Our souls long to be launched into some exciting exploit. Inside each of us is this incredible need to be significant, even heroic, ridding the earth of evil villains who perpetrate their devious plots on helpless people.

Or it could be that you yearn to live out some romantic love affair like Solomon and the Shulamite woman—an unbridled passion lived out loud. Maybe you feel an unquenchable thirst to be pursued by a lover so taken by your beauty that he braves every obstacle to win you over. Or perhaps you want to be the nobleman who, captivated by the king's daughter, must triumphantly gain her love. I could use thousands of scenarios to describe the divine passion that is like carbonated soda bottled deep inside the soul of every Christian. Life's circumstances shake us up until we feel as though we are going to explode on the scene with the zeal of Christ, turning over the tables of unrighteousness and releasing the Kingdom into the darkest places of the planet.

Yet when the curtain begins to close on our life's drama, many of us are left with a boring script about a monotonous journey filled with carefully planned, riskless days that we have somehow managed to exchange for the Great Adventure. There we sit on the porch of life with our strategically thought-out retirement plan, created with the help of our wise, professional stewards . . . yet all the while we are waiting for life to start. We have car insurance, house insurance, unemployment insurance, life insurance, fire insurance, earthquake insurance, dental insurance, loss of income insurance, not to mention that every appliance in our house is insured. We have 100,000-mile car warranties and extended warranties on our iPhones. We are the most overprotected and underchallenged people in history. We live twenty years longer than our great-grandfathers or great-grandmothers did, but we are literally bored to death.

I am convinced that our passion is being siphoned off as we sit on our couches, brainlessly watching some actor, actress or athlete live out the life we long for on the boob tube! We spend our days talking about the movies we have watched instead of the experiences we have had. Our kids do not even go outside to play anymore. Instead, they sit in front of the Xbox and play video games for hours on end, wasting their superhero dreams on some virtual reality screen that sedates them through some high-score deception into believing that they have really saved the world.

Then there are always the "helicopter" moms and/or dads who are so overprotective and controlling of their children that they hover over the kids' every move so that they do not skin up their fragile little souls in the game of life. We used to teach our kids that "all day, all night . . . angels are watching over me, my Lord," but our overprotected culture has caused a cosmic unemployment crisis in the heavenlies.

Understand that I am not opposed to movies, video games, insurance or wise parenting, but when we exchange our God-given craving for adventure . . . when we exchange a faith-filled life in the jungle for watching some cotton candy circus clown, we have lost sight of our divine destiny.

It is true that adventure comes at a price. There are real reasons why people choose not to leave their comfort zone for the call of the wild. You could die trying to walk out your mission, or suffer some great loss in the midst of your pursuit. And I am not saying that you should not be careful at times. But Christians simply were never designed to live in a bubble or drive a tank back and forth to work.

You were born again by faith. God gave you a blank document and said, "Sign on the dotted line, and I'll fill in the contract later." You sign, then you notice that the Holy Spirit signed the bottom of the contract, too, on the line that said "*Comforter*." It seldom occurs to us, however, that we are supposed to live our lives in such a way that we will need one!

Some folks are ignorant of what they got themselves into when they asked Christ into their lives. You can pick these baffled believers out of a crowd because their prayers sound something like, "Here kitty, kitty, kitty." They are stunned when the Lion of the tribe of Judah emerges out from behind the door, with a roar that would raise the dead! Then they spend most of their lives trying to domesticate and potty train the big cat, hoping to control their own destiny. But until you stick your head in the mouth of the Lion, you have not really seen the depths of the Kingdom! Jesus put it this way: "For whoever wishes to save his life will lose it, but whoever loses his life for My sake, he is the one who will save it" (Luke 9:24, NASB).

The only real way to enjoy the born-again experience is to give up trying *not* to die, and to give in to the yearning inside you to cross over the chicken line! Whether it is Abraham at over one hundred years old braving Mount Moriah to sacrifice Isaac, or Daniel experiencing the lions' den, or David taunting the giant, or Esther defying death by approaching the king, or Joshua marching on Jericho, or Gideon's army of three hundred pitcher-carrying soldiers, the moral of the story remains the same—life begins only after death has done its part!

Tracy was not born with supernatural genes. She just refuses to reduce her life down to the level of her fear. Many people will tell you that they are not afraid of anything, but the truth is that they have reduced their life to adapt to their fear. For example, if I am afraid to fly and never get on a plane, I do not "feel" the emotion of fear because I have reduced my life to accommodate it.

The only thing keeping you from being the next Nelson Mandela, Abraham Lincoln, Esther, David, Joshua or some other mighty man or woman of God is fear! You must conquer it or it will steal your destiny, rob you of your God-given exploits and destroy your offspring. Fear is an equal-opportunity destroyer. Everyone in the world has faced fear at some point in his or her life. But as Dr. Mark Chironna, senior pastor of the Master's Touch International Church in Orlando, says, "My destiny is in need of me!" When we focus on our call in life instead of on our apprehensions, a sort of Holy Spirit vortex seems to form around us that sucks us into a celestial boot camp and then catapults us over the top of our wailing wall, into our supernatural assignment.

Courage never comes on the couch! Waiting until you have enough courage to meet the challenges that your mission requires is like sitting at home watching football games on TV and wondering when the scouts are going to recognize your talent and put *you* in the game. Like the ten lepers who were healed on the way to see the priest, it is only as we make our way to the battlefield that we find the courage to engage our enemy.

So what is it going to be? Wouldn't you rather die in faith than live in doubt? I wonder how many people say to themselves on their deathbed, "I wish I hadn't led such an adventurous life. I should have played it safer."

I love what Winston Churchill said: "History will be kind to me for I intend to write it." If someone shot a documentary of your life now, would anyone want to watch it? Is there enough adventure in your entire life that Hollywood could at least keep people entertained for two hours with your story?

Some years ago as I was lying on the floor praying, I heard God say, "Write your obituary and work backward; then people won't have to lie about you at your funeral."

There is only one way I know of to ensure that you live to the outer limits of your destiny: Hang around with people who scare you! Jason and I wrote this book because we are the product of Tracy's courage. Having her live at our house for so many years was like renting a room to one of David's mighty men and then trying to convince ourselves that we were radicals. Tracy would come home from one of her "night strikes" (or better yet, bring a street person home with her) and share her exploits with us at the dinner table. Our hearts would be stirred like a caged lion scratching at the door of freedom, longing to break the leash of domestication and rush back into the jungle to experience the supernatural life that God had planned for us.

It is our desire that Tracy's life would have the same dangerous effect on your heart that it has had on ours. May your soul be ravished for the Great Adventure!

Tracy Evans is a physician assistant who has served as a Christian medical missionary in 64 nations over the past 30 years. She establishes clinics and ministries in Muslim and Communist developing nations and in countries recovering from war or natural disasters. Currently she has a registered ministry, iReachAfrica, in postwar Mozambique. This ministry has built a baby clinic, a feeding program and a hospice/ recovery center and currently serves 900 orphan infants and HIV-positive children, plus their caregivers.

Tracy and her co-workers at iReachAfrica have also planted 21 churches, built a preschool/ kindergarten and developed two prison ministries. In addition, they host leadership seminars for government officials and pastors. For more information, see the new ministry website www.iReachAfrica.org or contact Tracy at ireachafrica@gmail.com.

Kris Vallotton has been happily married to his wife, Kathy, for 36 years. They have four children and eight grandchildren. Three of their children are in full-time vocational ministry. Kris is the co-founder and senior overseer of the Bethel School of Supernatural Ministry, which has grown to more than thirteen hundred full-time students in thirteen years. He is also the founder and president of Moral Revolution, an organization dedicated to cultural transformation.

Kris is the senior associate leader of Bethel Church in Redding, California, and has served with Bill Johnson for more than 33 years. He has written and co-authored numerous books, and his revelatory insight and humorous delivery make him a much sought after international conference speaker.

You can contact Kris or find out more about his other ministry materials at www.kvministries.com, or you can follow Kris and Kathy on their Facebook fan page at www.facebook.com/kvministries.

**Jason Vallotton** was born and raised in Weaverville, California, a small town known for its mountainous views and mellow pace. He got a quick start in life, marrying his high school sweetheart at the age of 18 and fathering their three children, Elijah, Rilie and Evan, by the age of 24.

Jason's life has been riddled with challenges, from raising a young family and fighting fires through the hills of Northern California to overcoming the heartbreak of having his marriage dissolve in 2008. He has become a testimony to the redemptive power of perseverance and unconditional love.

Jason's love for people and his drive to see them completely whole has led him to Redding, California, where he lives with his wife, Lauren, and the children, and where he helps oversee Bethel School of Supernatural Ministry and a men's sexual purity group. Having gone through the hardships of life and come out on the other side, Jason has a heart to see people restored to complete wholeness and freedom, the way God intended them to be.

# Other Books by Kris Vallotton

*Developing a Supernatural Lifestyle:*
*A Practical Guide to a Life of Signs,*
*Wonders, and Miracles*

*Heavy Rain:*
*Renew the Church, Transform the World*

*Moral Revolution:*
*The Naked Truth about Sexual Purity*

*Spirit Wars:*
*Winning the Invisible Battle*
*against Sin and the Enemy*

*The Supernatural Power of Forgiveness:*
*Discover How to Escape Your Prison of*
*Pain and Unlock a Life of Freedom*
*(co-authored with Jason Vallotton)*

*The Supernatural Ways of Royalty:*
*Discovering Your Rights and Privileges of*
*Being a Son or Daughter of God*
*(co-authored with Bill Johnson)*

*Basic Training for the Supernatural*
*Ways of Royalty (workbook)*

*Basic Training for the Prophetic Ministry*
*(workbook)*

# More Spiritual Inspiration from Kris Vallotton

You know the battle is raging—but are you fighting the right enemy?

Sharing his deeply personal story of demonic bondage, torment and deliverance, pastor Kris Vallotton turns the idea of spiritual warfare as we know it on its head. He reveals the diabolical lies and strategies of the enemy—attacks and traps so subtle and deceptive that we may find our souls and hearts imprisoned without even knowing it. But you can win the battle against sin and the enemy. Victory is within your grasp. Will you take hold?

*Spirit Wars*
by Kris Vallotton

chosenbooks.com